The Fiber Rich Kitchen Cookbook

Linda Moskovics

AuthorHouse™
1663 Liberty Drive
Bloomington, IN 47403
www.authorhouse.com
Phone: 1 (800) 839-8640

Published by AuthorHouse 03/27/2017

ISBN: 978-1-5246-5243-2 (sc)
978-1-5246-5244-9 (e)

Library of Congress Control Number: 2016921625

Print information available on the last page.

This book is printed on acid-free paper.

authorHOUSE®

CONTENTS

Preface

Food has always fascinated me.

Watching Grandma Sophie create tantalizing cookies and dishes like crackling, succulent duck paired with juicy sweet-and-sour red cabbage intrigued me. Wonderful aromas always wafted from Grandma's kitchen; her creations begged to be eaten. She was truly my inspiration, and she ignited my romance with food and my obsession with recipes.

My mother helped to further my preoccupation with food by allowing me to play and experiment in her kitchen while I was growing up. Home economics classes also fueled my desire to explore and create healthy, delicious dishes. Trying recipes and improving them by making healthier and tastier versions has been my passion and hobby for years.

The diet of today's society is sorely lacking in fiber, and this is wreaking havoc with people's health and well-being. Lack of fiber causes major health issues and is a contributor to today's tragic obesity and diabetes epidemic, especially among children. It is estimated that by 2030, 50 percent of the citizens of the United States will have diabetes.

For years, I have been on a quest to create quick, easy, and tasty fiber-rich dishes made from easily located ingredients. In addition, dealing with my own digestive issues has prompted me to research and experiment with food, and this cookbook is a culmination of my efforts. The recipes in this book are designed to be quick, easy, healthy, and delicious; most of them are chock-full of life-supporting fiber.

Planning meals reduces stress for me. If I have meals planned in advance and the necessary groceries for the meals purchased, I don't have to worry about what to cook for lunch, dinner, or the entire week—or even longer, thanks to leftovers. I have been doing this practice ever since I was a young newlywed.

I hope you enjoy preparing and eating my recipes as much as I have loved creating them. After a good home-cooked meal, my father would always say, "I raise my glass to home cooking." Today, I say, "I raise my glass to fiber-rich cooking."

A special thank-you from the bottom of my heart goes out to all my recipe testers/tasters (also known as my "guinea pigs"): Vanassa Goodman, Amy and Marshall Zeidell and family, and Judy Shafer. Most importantly, I wish to thank Ray Bronco, who has been my biggest encourager to write this cookbook but also my strongest critic. You all have heard me talk about my dream of writing a cookbook for many years. Well, now it is finally done—and I could not have done it without your help. There is no safe way to write a cookbook without honest tasters, and I could not possibly have tasted and eaten all that food by myself.

The rest is up to those who are inclined to pick up a copy of my cookbook. Venture forth and try a recipe and perhaps a new food. Better health and good food await those who do.

Discussion about Fiber

The focus of this cookbook is to provide tasty, easy, and quick fiber-rich recipes utilizing grains, legumes, beans, fruits, vegetables, and other fiber-rich foods that are easily obtained locally. These recipes should appeal to a wide variety of palettes, both among adults and children. The recipes are perfect for anyone wishing to eat or cook the fiber-rich way and spend less time in food preparation. Most of the dishes can be easily packed to carry in a lunch box or cooler. Bottom line: many people are overweight and don't consume enough fiber.

Disclaimer: There are many different opinions on nutrition. My idea of fiber-rich recipes is just one of them. Thus, for the reader, use what you like and what works for you! These recipes may appear to be on the mild side, not too spicy or full of peppers. This is due to my personal preference. Just add more seasonings, peppers, or both to spice up the recipes to your liking. Remember: recipes are just guidelines to follow, merely words on a page or screen. Your personal judgment is your best friend. Trust your senses, intuition, and taste buds to make any changes that modify the dish to your liking. When a recipe calls for a specific ingredient, feel free to add more, add less, leave it out, or substitute a different ingredient or seasoning. Taste as you proceed, and make adjustments to your liking. Cook a dish long enough to meld the flavors but not so long that it turns to slop.

Get out of the rut of eating the same foods over and over. Expand your culinary interests. Try some new grains. Experiment with these recipes and ingredients; there is a huge selection of dishes you can cook that are fiber rich. Use these recipes to try foods that are new and different but also incredibly healthy for you. Always check with your health care provider before increasing the intake of fiber in your diet and find out what the correct amount is for you.

What is all this hype about fiber? What is fiber?

We all need fiber in our diets in order to be healthy and thrive. New reasons for eating fiber are being discovered all the time. Having a fiber-rich diet means using foods and products in their whole, natural state or foods that have been processed as little as possible to retain their fiber content. The closer a food is to its natural state, the more it contains those nutrients that feed the gut-friendly bacteria.

It is often a struggle for most people to know what to eat in order to get more fiber in their diets. Picking up fast food or ready-cooked food or going to a restaurant is easier for most people. But with a little advanced planning, the recipes in this cookbook can be assembled or cooked ahead and thus be available for eating anytime. You won't have to decide at the last minute what to eat or grab something unhealthy. Personally, I tire of eating the same foods often. In an effort to eat a healthier, fiber-rich diet myself, I have created, tested, and compiled these fiber-rich recipes with the fiber-conscious individual in mind.

Eating a fiber-rich diet should be and can be pleasurable. A fiber-rich diet includes abundant fruits, vegetables, cereals in their natural states; legumes, grains, and beans; and less meat, poultry, and dairy products. Most people do not know where to find fiber-rich recipes that also taste good. I have compiled some conveniently in one handy cookbook that is divided into categories.

Since I am not a scientist and this is a cookbook, I will include only a very short discussion of fiber.

Some Beneficial Properties of Fiber

Fiber benefits and is important to our health. It is also known as roughage or bulk. Fiber is found in many of the superfoods. Eating sufficient fiber

- promotes a feeling of fullness that aids in weight control and can help people reach and maintain a healthy weight;

- helps lower blood cholesterol levels by trapping cholesterol and fats;

- can help ease IBS (irritable bowel syndrome);

- can help prevent or minimize constipation by promoting regularity and elimination;

- lowers the risk of hemorrhoids;

- may reduce the risk of certain types of cancer;

- can ward off intestinal conditions like diverticulosis;

- may improve blood pressure;

- slows the absorption of sugars, which may improve blood-glucose control and lower the risk for diabetes;

- causes fermentation and promotes the growth of healthy bacteria; and

- may lower the risk for heart attack and stroke.

Research suggests that more than 90 percent of Americans are not meeting their daily fiber requirement. The National Fiber Council reports that most people consume only about 10–15 grams per day. The amount of fiber you need depends on your age and gender. According to the American Journal of Medicine issue of October 9, 2013, men should eat 30–38 grams of fiber a day while women need 21–25 grams. The American Heart Association recommends at least 25–30 grams of dietary fiber per day for the general adult population; that's about six times the amount of fiber in an average serving of oatmeal.

Fiber is the key to feeling full on fewer calories; increased fiber curbs appetite and boosts a feeling of fullness. Fiber increases levels of the hormone leptin, which can increase the feeling of satiety or fullness. Therefore, eating more fiber may lead to a reduction in calorie intake.

Fiber is known to boost metabolism because the body works hard to digest the fiber; this in turn burns calories. Fiber passes through the body without being digested and is eliminated. It can aid elimination by absorbing water, thus helping to prevent constipation and ease irritable bowel syndrome. It can also help ward off intestinal conditions like diverticulosis, and it lowers the risk of hemorrhoids. Blood pressure might be improved as well. It is also believed that high-fiber foods may help to prevent inflammation; this is an internal process that can accelerate the aging process. A healthful diet includes fiber from a variety of sources rather than from one single source, such as bran. A high-fiber diet makes sense, especially when you consider the benefits of eating foods in as natural a state as you can.

A fiber-rich diet aids a healthy digestive system. Intestinal bacteria love fiber and use it as a food source. A diet high in fiber helps the good bacteria to grow and protects you from the harmful bacteria. Fiber and cancer studies conducted at various scientific facilities around the world show a definite connection between eating a high-fiber diet and a lessened risk of contracting many kinds of cancer. The FDA allows a food to be labeled a "good source" of fiber if the food contains 2.5 to 4.9 grams of fiber per serving; a food can be labeled an "excellent source" of fiber if it contains more than 4.9 grams per serving.

There is much talk today about prebiotics. Prebiotics are food for probiotics. The prebiotics pass through your stomach and small intestine. Then they stimulate the growth of the good bacteria in the large intestine. Interestingly, prebiotics are found in high-fiber vegetables like asparagus, onions, leaks, garlic, and artichokes; legumes such as lentils, red kidney beans, and chickpeas; and fruits like grapefruit, bananas, and watermelon (Better Homes and Gardens, June 2015, 160).

According to David Perlmutter, MD, and Kristin Loberg in their book *Brain Maker*, a prebiotic must have three characteristics: it must be nondigestible, it must be able to be fermented or metabolized by the intestinal bacteria, and this fermentation or metabolizing must confer health benefits. They state, "We've all heard about the benefits of eating fiber. It turns out that the effects of dietary fiber on the growth of healthy bacteria in the gut may well be fiber's most important aspect" (194).

Fiber refers to the parts of plant foods such as fruits, vegetables, and grains that cannot be digested in the human body. Your body does not digest and absorb fiber. There are two types of dietary fiber: insoluble and soluble. Both types of fiber are important and provide benefits.

Insoluble fiber (nonfermentable fiber) does not dissolve in water. It hastens the movement of food through the body as it travels through the stomach and small intestine. It's like sweeping your gut, thereby decreasing the risk of some cancers. It also adds bulk to the stool and promotes regularity. Examples of insoluble fiber include the skins of many vegetables and fruits. Each gram of insoluble fiber ingested will sweep away about 6 calories. Insoluble fiber is found in foods such as wheat bran; whole grains and whole-grain products; whole wheat products, like whole wheat flour; brown rice; nuts; seeds; some vegetables, like green peas, green beans, carrots, cauliflower, potatoes, celery, corn, popcorn, cucumbers, tomatoes, and zucchini; and dried fruit, like prunes and raisins.

Soluble (viscous) fiber dissolves in water. It breaks down as it passes through your digestive track, absorbing water as it forms a gel that helps to stabilize blood sugar levels. It slows the movement of food through the digestive tract. It has been found to lower blood cholesterol and help regulate blood glucose. Soluble fiber is found in some vegetables, like asparagus, kale, potatoes, broccoli, okra, cabbage, and carrots; certain fruits, like apples, citrus fruits, blueberries, pears, strawberries, figs, oranges, plums, and rhubarb; legumes, like dried beans, lentils, and peas; the brans of various cereals, like oats, rice, barley, and corn; nuts; seeds; and psyllium, which is a natural supplement made from the seed of a shrub-like herb.

It is very important to increase your intake of fiber gradually over several weeks, as a sudden increase in fiber consumption may cause extreme discomfort, including bloating and gas. It is also very important to increase your fluid intake with an increase in fiber consumption to prevent constipation and assist with the processing of the fiber while your body adapts.

Choose foods that naturally contain fiber. Adding fiber to your diet is easy, as there are many good sources of fiber. Simply eat more plant foods like those listed above. Fruits and vegetables should be eaten unpeeled and washed in order for you to consume their maximum dietary fiber. Buying organic is the best option, because if we assume that organic foods were grown without the use of pesticides, this would make it safer to eat the skins and peels than with nonorganic foods.

There is another class of fiber called functional fibers. These are made from natural or synthetic ingredients. In order to increase fiber content, they are added to some packaged foods. Examples of these functional fibers include resistant starch, cellulose gum, chicory root, psyllium, and inulin. These functional fibers may provide a health benefit by slowing the rise of glucose in the blood or by increasing bulk. Research has shown it is better to consume fiber from a variety of whole-food sources, such as vegetables, fruits, and whole grains, rather than processed foods with fiber additives or functional fibers.

Grains

Grain refers to food-related grasses and their fruits or seeds. The extent to which the grains are processed determines their fiber content, which can be quite significant. Today it is easy to find unusual, whole ancient grains. Ancient grains have been around for thousands of years. Cereals and grains should be purchased in their natural or unrefined state as much as possible, since through processing, the fiber may be lost. Whole grains are digested more slowly than refined grains. This helps to maintain consistent blood sugar levels, which helps feelings of fullness last longer. This can curb cravings for sweets and snacks and may prevent the inflammation that increases cancer risk. Some grains are gluten free. Grains are filling and can serve as the foundation for any nutritious, heart-healthy, easy-to-make dish. A hearty grain salad packed with vegetables is a meal with both protein and fiber.

Uncooked whole grains keep a long time. Store them in an airtight, sealed container. Refrigerate leftover cooked grains. They will keep about a week in a covered container. For longer storage of cooked grains, put them in the freezer. Grains are versatile. They can pick up flavors from whatever liquid they are cooked in or whatever ingredients they are mixed with.

Cooking methods and times for the various grains are not included in this cookbook. There are various methods that can be used to cook grains. You can easily look these up yourself in another cookbook, on the Internet, or on the grain packaging and choose the best method for your purposes.

I have tried to include recipes for many different grains. For many of the recipes, the grains can be eaten cold for lunch as a salad or as a healthy light dinner. Some of the grains can be exchanged for others in the various recipes provided here with similar, satisfying results. I encourage you to experiment with the different grains; try new tastes and have fun. Learn to cook these grains in creative ways and learn how to substitute them for your usual standbys. To get you started, here is a brief overview of some of the most popular of these high-fiber whole grains:

Amaranth: a tiny, yellow, ancient grain of the Aztecs. Technically, it is not a grain but the fruit (seed) of a plant. It's a great source of insoluble fiber with about 8 grams of fiber per cooked cup. It can be bought as a whole grain, as flour, or as rolled flakes. It has a nutty flavor and is gluten free. It can have a fine crunch or a porridge-like texture depending on how it is cooked. It goes well with honey and makes a comforting high-protein breakfast cereal or a great side dish. It is best stored in the refrigerator.

Barley: an ancient grain rich in both soluble and insoluble fiber. It comes in both hulled and pearled varieties. Whole-hulled barley (barley groats) has had the outermost hull removed and is higher in fiber than pearled barley. Whole-grain hulled barley has more fiber than any other whole grain. It has soluble fiber, which may reduce LDL cholesterol. Pearled barley has had both its outer layer and its bran removed. Barley has a chewy texture and a nutty flavor. Enjoy barley in a pilaf, add it to soup, or eat it for a great breakfast mixed with fruit, yogurt, nuts, and cinnamon.

Brown Rice: the whole grain or rice with only the outer husk removed. It has three times the fiber of white rice. It comes in short-, medium-, and long-grain varieties. The rice bran, which remains in brown rice, may lower cholesterol. Brown rice is more slowly digested than processed white rice. It has many culinary uses.

Buckwheat: the gluten-free fruit or seed of a plant that is related to rhubarb. It is sold as groats, grits, or flour. Buckwheat groats contain important vitamins and minerals. They can be substituted for rice or barley in some recipes. Roasted buckwheat groats are known as *kasha* in Eastern Europe. Store buckwheat in a sealed container in a cool, dark location. It contains soluble fiber and is protein rich and gluten free.

Bulgur: a type of cracked wheat kernel that has been precooked and then dried. The resulting grain is slightly chewy with a mild flavor. It is often used in salads, like tabbouleh, and is a Middle Eastern staple. Bulgur is a great source of fiber, with about 8 grams per cup. It is high in slow-digesting carbohydrates and can help keep your digestive tract healthy. It can be found ground coarse, medium, and fine. Pilaf, or stuffing, is made from coarse-ground bulgur; medium-ground bulgur is used to make cereals; and fine-ground bulgur is used for tabbouleh. Bulgur lends its nutty flavor to whatever it is combined with. Store bulgur in the refrigerator; it will keep for a long time. It can be used in place of rice in many recipes

Corn: the most-produced grain worldwide. It is gluten free and has a high ratio of insoluble to soluble fiber. Corn can support the growth of friendly bacteria, as its fiber nourishes the lower digestive tract. It is also a source of several vitamins.

Farro: an ancient form of wheat that resembles barley and has a subtle nutty flavor. It comes whole, semipearled, or pearled. Whole farro can take an hour to cook. Soak for at least 3 hours or overnight to reduce cooking time. It is similar to spelt and can be eaten hot or cold and in soups, pilaf, salads, or wraps.

Freekeh: an ancient grain from young, green wheat that has been toasted to bring out nuttiness and crunch. It comes either whole or cracked. It is high in fiber and protein.

Oat: a truly healthy grain that is high in both soluble and insoluble fiber, protein, and manganese. Oats are most famous for oatmeal and cookies.

Millet: a nutritious, gluten-free grain that is a staple of the diets of large portions of the world, including Africa and Asia. It is a good source of protein and is rich in fiber. It has no characteristic flavor of its own; it tends to take on the flavor of foods prepared with it.

Quinoa: the ancient "mother grain" of the Incas. It is not a grain but a seed, a complete protein that contains all essential amino acids. It is high in minerals, high in fiber, and gluten free, and it cooks quickly. Rinsing the quinoa well before cooking eliminates the bitter coating of saponin. It comes in several colors and can be eaten hot or cold. There are many uses for quinoa; it can be eaten as a side dish; in a salad, casserole, or dessert; for breakfast with fruit, spices, and milk or yogurt; alone; and in numerous other ways.

Rye: a high-protein grain that is a good source of fiber. Whole-rye foods can help with blood sugar control, due to their high fiber content.

Sorghum: a whole-grain, high-fiber food that is a dietary staple in India and Africa. It is nutritious and gluten free and has a hearty, chewy texture. Being versatile, it is great for salads and pilafs and can also be popped like popcorn.

Spelt: an ancient form of wheat high in fiber that some people sensitive to wheat can tolerate. It comes in both refined and whole-grain forms. It is mildly sweet, chewy, nutty, and slightly buttery with a texture similar to barley but not as starchy.

Teff: an ancient grain that is extremely nutritious. It has been a staple in northern Africa for centuries. The grains are very tiny and come in ivory or reddish brown. When cooked, Teff is moist, and its flavor is both sweet and bitter; it is said to make a delicious breakfast cereal.

Triticale: a new grain that was created by crossing durum wheat and rye. It can be found as whole berries, rolled like oats, or ground into flour.

Whole Wheat: a very good source of dietary fiber, manganese, and magnesium in its original form. It is made into flour and widely used in baking and for cereals.

Wheat Berries: have a nutty, sweet flavor and a crisp, chewy texture. They may be used in soups, stews, salads, and pilafs. They must be soaked overnight before cooking.

Legumes

Legumes are a source of plant protein and are high in fiber. The majority of legumes are improved by being simmered with fragrant, or sweet-smelling, items such as onions, garlic, shallots, chilies, and herbs, like thyme, sage, bay leaves, parsley, and so on. There is a vast variety of legumes to explore. They can provide versatile, easy, and low-cost meals year round. In addition, the phytochemicals in legumes might lower the risk of cancer if consumed several times a week.

There are several recipes in this cookbook using legumes. This family includes dried beans, peas, and lentils. On average, cooked legumes contain about 6 grams of fiber per 1/2-cup serving. Legumes can easily be added to a diet. Many soups, stews, chilis, salads, casseroles, and sandwich spreads feature legumes. They can be eaten alone or mixed in dishes, where they are known to absorb the flavors of the other ingredients

Beans

Beans are abundant and possess both types of healthy fiber and resistant starch. This helps to control and stabilize blood sugar and help keep weight down. Beans have also been known to lower cholesterol. You can use canned beans or you can cook dried beans. One can of beans equals approximately 2 cups of cooked dried beans. Since beans are often bland tasting by themselves, they can be versatile; it is often possible to substitute different varieties in any recipe that calls for beans. Combining beans with grains or seeds can provide complete proteins.

Nuts

Eat nuts in place of foods high in saturated fats and calories. Eat only about 1/3 cup (1 oz.) per day as they are high in calories. Sprinkle them on cereal, yogurt, salads, pasta, rice, stir fries, use in crusts or be creative.

Examples of high-fiber foods

Even though it is easy to locate lists of foods high in fiber online or in books and magazines, I have included several examples. Many fruits and vegetables are high in fiber. It is not necessary to provide an endless list, but some are better sources than others.

Fruits: raspberries (raw), blackberries (raw), boysenberries (raw), figs (dried), dates, prunes, pears, kiwi, kumquats, oranges, persimmons, guava, tangerines, and avocados

Vegetables: artichokes, beets and beet greens, green peas, spinach, winter squash, broccoli, turnip greens, brussels sprouts, carrots, jicama, corn, pumpkin, kale, lima beans, okra, parsnips, and sweet potatoes and yams

Whole Grains (with more than 3 grams of fiber per serving): amaranth, barley, bran, bulgur, quinoa, whole wheat, oats, brown rice, and popcorn

Legumes: navy beans, split peas, lentils, pinto beans, black beans, kidney beans, white beans, black eyed peas, and lima beans

Nuts: almonds, pistachios, and pecans

Seeds: chia, flax, pinon nuts, and sesame

Good health to you, reader. Go ahead, and try a fiber-rich diet! You won't be sorry.

Breakfast or Morning Meal

Breakfast (or as some call it, the "morning meal") is often promoted as the most important meal of the day. There are numerous foods that people consider breakfast foods. Many are quick to cook, but some are not.

Many of the ancient grains tend to be overlooked as morning meals or breakfast foods, but they can be cooked into stellar hot cereal. Oats cooked into oatmeal are the most common and popular. Some examples of these other excellent breakfast grains include barley, quinoa, farro, spelt, teff, freekeh, amaranth, and buckwheat groats. The grains are nutty, toothsome, and delicious. Like porridge, they simply need to be cooked to your desired texture. They can be cooked in water, milk, juice, or a combination of liquids. Serve them as you typically would oatmeal. Any can be topped with milk, fresh fruit, dried fruit, nuts, yogurt, kefir, ricotta cheese, spices (such as cinnamon or nutmeg), chia seeds, flaxseeds, honey, maple syrup, brown sugar, and more. The options are limited only by your taste and imagination.

Recipes follow for barley, quinoa, millet, and a buckwheat combo. Try some of the other grains mentioned above; experiment with combinations of the various grains. Depending on your taste preferences, many of these grains would be a delicious way to start your day. My Oatmeal in a Pan is a different way to enjoy cooked oatmeal.

Eating a fiber-rich breakfast with cooked grains is a good way to jump-start your fiber intake for the day. The fiber will help keep you feeling full and satisfied longer.

Basic Oatmeal

Oatmeal is considered by many to be a stellar fiber-rich breakfast. Steel-cut oats are preferable, but old-fashioned oats are good too. Please stay away from instant and flavored varieties, as they have less nutrition.

My significant other likes his oats very creamy, so I add extra water and cook the oats a little longer; they come out smooth and moist. For a taste change, substitute a nondairy milk (such as almond milk) for the water. My daughter, who has a baby, likes her steel-cut oats ready when she wakes up. She puts them in a tiny slow cooker with water, sets it on warm, and lets the mixture cook all night; her oatmeal is done when she wakes up.

Here are the basic proportions for one serving of oatmeal:

> Old-fashioned oats: 1 cup water to 1/2 cup oats

> Steel-cut oats: 1 cup water to 1/4 cup oats

Just add some fiber-rich fruit or nuts to your oatmeal, and you will have started your day the fiber-rich way.

Hint: Try the Oatmeal in a Pan for my delicious alternate version of oats.

Oatmeal in a Pan

This method gives the oatmeal a lighter texture and a sweet, crisp crust. Everyone will love it, and it is fiber-rich too.

Makes 8 or more servings

- 2 cups old-fashioned rolled oats (not quick or instant)
- 1/2 cup chopped nuts of choice, divided
- 1 teaspoon baking powder
- 1 teaspoon ground cinnamon
- 1/2 teaspoon ground nutmeg
- zest of one lemon or orange to taste
- 2 cups milk or non-dairy milk of choice (may need a bit more)
- 1/3–1/2 cup sugar or brown sugar, depending on sweetness desired
- 1 large egg
- 2 tablespoons butter or margarine, melted
- 1 tablespoon lemon juice or orange juice
- 2 teaspoons vanilla extract
- 2 ripe bananas, peeled and cut into 1/2-inch slices
- 2 cups fresh or frozen blueberries, divided (other berries may be substituted)

Preheat oven to 350 degrees F. Coat an 8-inch or 9-inch square baking dish with cooking spray.

In a bowl, combine oats, baking powder, nutmeg, cinnamon, citrus zest, and 1/4 cup nuts.

In another bowl, whisk together butter or margarine, milk, sugar, egg, vanilla extract, and citrus juice.

Arrange sliced bananas in a single layer on the bottom of the prepared dish. Sprinkle 1 1/2 cups berries over the banana, reserving the remaining 1/2 cup for the topping.

Sprinkle the oat mixture over the fruit. Drizzle the liquid mixture over the oats, making sure the milk penetrates through the oats. Scatter remaining berries and nuts over the top.

Bake 35–45 minutes, or until the top and edges are golden and the center has set. If desired, sprinkle with a little more sugar or drizzle some maple syrup over the top. Cut pieces of whatever size you desire and serve.

Three options to make this recipe ahead of time:

1. Combine the wet and dry ingredients in separate bowls. When ready to bake, assemble as directed and bake.

2. Assemble the entire dish, let it sit overnight, and bake it in the morning for a softer texture.

3. Bake the night before and reheat when serving.

Other versions: Instead of berries and bananas, get creative! Stir raisins, craisins, chopped dates, chopped figs, or other dried fruit into the oatmeal mixture before baking.

Barley for Breakfast

Breakfast is the perfect time to enjoy this delicious, unusual, and fiber-packed grain.

Makes 3–4 servings

- 1/2 cup barley (pearl or hull-less)
- 3 cups water, milk, non-dairy milk of choice, or juice (or a combination thereof)
- 2–3 apples, pears, or other fruit; washed, cored (if necessary), and coarsely chopped
- 1/8 cup honey, brown sugar, or maple syrup (if desired)
- 1/2 teaspoon ground nutmeg
- 1/4 teaspoon ground cinnamon
- 1/4 teaspoon ground clove
- splash of vanilla extract
- spices, such as ginger (optional)
- lemon juice or orange juice (optional)

Place barley, liquid, and fruit in a medium pot and bring to a boil.

Cover and simmer for 40 minutes, or until the barley is tender.

Add spices, sweetener, vanilla extract, and citrus juice (if using). Simmer 5 minutes. Mixture will thicken as it cooks.

This is delicious topped with yogurt, kefir, and chia seeds. Be creative!

Hot Breakfast Millet

You can make this thick or soupy. You will discover what you like by experimenting.

Makes 1-2 servings

- 1/3 cup raw millet*
- 1 cup water, milk, non-dairy milk of choice, juice, or a combination* (add more water or liquid if necessary for a more porridge like consistency)
- 1 teaspoon ground cinnamon
- dash of nutmeg
- splash of vanilla extract
- 2 tablespoons yogurt, milk, or kefir for added creaminess (optional)
- fruit and nuts for topping
- *To cook 1/2 cup raw millet, increase water to 1 1/2 cups.

Rinse millet. Place with liquid in a medium pot and bring to a boil.

Turn heat down to low. Cover and simmer 15–20 minutes, or until millet is tender and cooked the way you like hot cereal.

Add cinnamon, nutmeg and vanilla. Stir in yogurt, milk, or kefir if using

Add fruit and nuts.

Return lid and allow mixture to stand with heat turned off to blend the flavors.

Serve hot or warm.

The raw millet can also be cooked in a rice cooker according to the manufacturer's directions.

Quinoa for Breakfast

A different way to try quinoa: breakfast with fiber and protein

Makes 2 larger servings or 3 smaller servings

- 1/2 cup quinoa
- 1 cup water, milk of your choice, or juice
- 1 teaspoon vanilla extract
- 1/2 teaspoon ground cinnamon
- 1/8 teaspoon ground nutmeg
- 1/8 teaspoon ground ginger (optional)
- 1 large unpeeled apple, cored and grated
- lemon zest and juice for a tarter flavor (optional)

Rinse quinoa well in a mesh strainer with cold water.

Bring the water, milk, or juice to a gentle boil in a medium pot. Slowly add rinsed quinoa. Reduce heat. Add spices and vanilla extract.

Simmer covered 15–20 minutes until the liquid is absorbed.

Add apple and cook approximately 30 seconds more.

Add lemon zest and lemon juice, if using.

Serve hot or cold.

Variations:

Instead of the apple, add some sliced or chopped strawberries, peaches, nectarines, bananas, raisins, or other fruit of your choice.

Top with some chopped nuts and yogurt or drizzle on some milk, honey, or maple syrup. Yummy!

Ingredients can also be assembled in a rice cooker and cooked that way.

Breakfast Combo

A unique, fiber-rich hot cereal. Try it for a different taste experience.

Makes 3–4 servings

- 2 1/2 cups water, milk, or nondairy milk of choice
- 1/2 cup buckwheat groats
- 1/2 cup steel cut oats

Place all ingredients in a medium pot.

Bring to a boil.

Reduce heat. Simmer covered approximately 20 minutes, stirring occasionally, until all of the liquid is absorbed.

Serve topped with fruit of choice, nuts, yogurt, kefir, ground cinnamon, or anything else you enjoy on your hot cereal.

Blueberry Oatmeal Pancakes

Delicious fiber-rich breakfast. The oats, flour, and blueberries are all excellent sources of fiber. The oats will help keep you full longer.

Makes approximately 10 delicious fiber-rich pancakes approximately 2-3 inches in size

- 1 cup milk or non-dairy milk of choice
- 1 tablespoon white vinegar
- 1/2 cup whole wheat flour or white whole wheat flour
- 1/2 cup old-fashioned oats (not instant or steel cut)
- 1 tablespoon brown sugar
- 1 teaspoon baking powder
- 3/4 teaspoon baking soda
- 1 teaspoon ground cinnamon
- 2 tablespoons oil of choice
- 1 large egg
- 1 cup blueberries, fresh or frozen thawed
- cooking spray

Add vinegar to milk and let set 10 minutes to sour it.

Meanwhile, combine flour, oats, brown sugar, baking powder, baking soda, and

cinnamon in a large bowl.

Beat together milk mixture, oil, and egg in a small bowl. Add to flour mixture, stirring just until smooth.

Gently add the blueberries.

Spray a pan or griddle with cooking spray and heat to medium heat. Spoon about 1/4 cup batter per pancake onto griddle or pan. Turn pancakes over when tops are covered with bubbles. Continue to cook until the bottoms are lightly brown.

Serve plain or with desired toppings.

Buckwheat Pancakes

This is a fiber-rich pancake. Buckwheat contains many phytonutrients that may contribute to blood sugar control. Delicious with fruit, syrup, yogurt, peanut butter, or almond butter.

Makes approximately 10 pancakes approximately 2 inches in size

- 1 cup buckwheat flour
- 1 tablespoon brown sugar (use more for a sweeter pancake)
- 1 tablespoon baking powder
- 1 1/2 teaspoons ground cinnamon
- 1/2 teaspoon baking soda
- pinch of ground nutmeg (optional)
- 1 cup nondairy milk or sour milk (made by placing one tablespoon white vinegar in 1 cup milk and letting sit 10 minutes)
- 1/4 cup plain low-fat greek yogurt or regular plain low-fat yogurt
- 1/4 cup applesauce, homemade or store bought
- 1 egg
- 1 tablespoon canola oil or oil of choice
- 1 teaspoon vanilla extract

Mix together buckwheat flour, brown sugar, baking powder, baking soda, cinnamon, and nutmeg. Add milk, yogurt, applesauce, egg, oil, and vanilla and mix until combined.

Coat frying pan or griddle with cooking spray, or use slight amount of oil, butter, or margarine.

Drop 1/4–1/3 cup of batter for each pancake. Cook until bubbles form, and then turn and cook 3 minutes on the other side until the bottoms are lightly brown.

Serve plain or with desired toppings.

Sweet Potato Pancakes

Sweet potatoes are an excellent source of fiber. These pancakes are delicious topped with mashed banana, nectarines, peaches, or applesauce. Or you can use your favorite topping

Makes approximately 10 pancakes 2 inches in size

- 1/2 cup cooked sweet potato, mashed (unpeeled, if organic)
- 1 egg
- 1/3 cup white whole wheat flour or flour of choice (cassava flour works well)
- 1 teaspoon ground cinnamon
- 1/2 teaspoon baking powder

- 1/3 cup milk of choice (may need a little more)
- 1 tablespoon butter, melted, *or* 1 tablespoon oil of choice
- pinch of ground nutmeg
- cooking spray, butter or oil for frying

Mix mashed sweet potato in a mixing bowl with the egg.

Stir in flour, baking powder, cinnamon and nutmeg if using.

Add milk and stir.

Stir in the melted butter or oil. Mixture will be thick and lumpy. If a thinner consistency is desired, add more milk before frying.

Spray skillet with cooking spray, or use slight amount of butter or oil. Preheat the skillet to medium heat.

Spoon approximately 1/3 cup batter for each pancake and cook until bubbles form on surface, approximately 2 minutes.

Turn the pancakes and cook another 2–3 minutes until desired doneness.

Pancakes freeze well. Pop them out of the freezer for a quick breakfast or nutritious snack.

Breakfast Burrito

Try a burrito for breakfast for a change. This is a high-fiber burrito that can be eaten for any meal; it can be made ahead and warmed up to fit any schedule.

Makes 3 large burritos

- small amount of oil of choice
- 1/2 cup chopped or torn fresh spinach or kale
- 1/3 cup chopped scallions
- 1/4 cup chopped parsley or cilantro
- 1/2 cup chopped fresh tomato
- 1/2 cup corn kernels, fresh or frozen
- 1/4 teaspoon chili powder
- 1/4 teaspoon ground cumin
- 1/4 teaspoon garlic powder
- 1/4 teaspoon each salt and pepper (optional)
- 3 eggs, slightly beaten
- 3 whole-grain or whole wheat tortillas
- 3/4–1 cup canned refried beans *or* cooked beans of choice, slightly mashed or pureed
- 3/4 cup cheese of choice (such as cheddar, jack, mozzarella, queso fresco), plus more to sprinkle on top

Heat oil in a large skillet over low-medium heat. Sauté scallions, parsley or cilantro, and spinach or kale until softened.

Stir in tomatoes and corn. Add spices and beaten eggs to the vegetable mixture and stir until the eggs are set. Set aside.

Divide beans evenly among the tortillas, spreading over the center of each. Top each with 1/3 of egg-vegetable mixture. Sprinkle 1/4 cup cheese over each tortilla.

Fold sides of tortillas in and lightly roll each into a burrito.

Burritos may be wrapped individually in plastic wrap or foil and refrigerated to be heated later.

To heat, place burritos seam side down in a skillet or onto a cookie sheet. Warm the burritos slowly in the skillet till heated through and the cheese melts, or bake in a 375-degree oven for 15–20 minutes.

Sprinkle on more cheese if desired. Serve with salsa, sliced avocado, sour cream, yogurt, or your favorite burrito toppings.

Broccoli Spinach Omelet Bake

This baked omelet dish is fiber-rich and looks pretty and appetizing. Great for a brunch or potluck.

Makes 4 servings

- 4 eggs
- 1/4 cup milk
- 1 cup chopped cooked fresh broccoli or frozen broccoli, thawed
- 1 cup fresh baby spinach leaves, torn *or* frozen chopped spinach, thawed and squeezed dry
- 1/2 cup cooked pinto beans *or* canned pinto beans, rinsed and drained
- 1/2 cup shredded cheddar or swiss cheese, divided (works with other cheese as well)
- 2 teaspoons dried onion flakes *or* 2 tablespoons chopped red onion

- 1 teaspoon garlic powder
- 1/2 teaspoon salt
- 1/2 teaspoon dried basil
- 1/4 teaspoon or more chili powder for more spice (optional)
- ground paprika to sprinkle on top
- cherry tomatoes halved to place on top of dish before putting in the oven

Preheat oven to 325 degrees F.

Beat eggs with milk until light and fluffy. Stir in the broccoli, spinach, beans, 1/4 cup cheese, onion, garlic powder, salt, basil, and chili powder (if using).

Spray an 8-inch square baking dish lightly with cooking spray.

Pour ingredients into baking dish. Arrange tomato halves on top. Sprinkle with remaining cheese and paprika.

Bake uncovered 25–30 minutes.

Serve as is, or top with salsa, if desired.

Recipe can be doubled and baked in a 13 by 9 by 2 inch pan for the same amount of time.

Fiber-filled Smoothie

It is easy to find delicious and healthy smoothie recipes today. Drinking smoothies is a great way to increase your fiber intake. Smoothies provide protein, vitamins, antioxidants, and minerals. They are easy, quick to make, convenient, satisfying, and portable, making them excellent on-the-go meals that can provide energy for a long time. Including vegetables is a good way to get your vegetable quota for the day. There are numerous combinations of fruits and vegetables you can try. Below is my favorite fiber-rich smoothie recipe.

Makes 1 very large serving or 2 average servings

- 1 cup milk, coconut milk, nut milk, green tea, water, juice, or liquid of choice
- 1 bunch fresh kale with stems removed *or* fresh spinach (one cup or less)
- 1/2 cup fresh or frozen strawberries
- 1/2 cup fresh or frozen blueberries
- 1/2 cup sliced carrots
- 1/2 cup sliced celery
- 1/2 cup sliced apples or pears, peeled or unpeeled
- 1/2 cup peeled and sliced cucumber
- 1/2 cup frozen banana
- 1/2 cup plain yogurt *or* plain greek yogurt
- 1 scoop protein powder (optional)
- 2 handfuls ice
- stevia or honey to taste
- chia seed, cocoa powder, frozen pineapple, or mango (optional)

Place all ingredients in blending device and blend until smooth. May need to add some additional liquid.

Soups

Basic Bean Soup

Quick, easy, and fiber smart!

Makes 4–6 servings

- 1 tablespoon olive oil or oil of choice
- 1 cup chopped onion
- 3/4 cup chopped carrots
- 3/4 cup chopped celery
- 2 large cloves of garlic, minced
- 4 cups broth or stock, chicken, beef or vegetable depending on your preference
- 2 cups cooked beans of choice *or* canned beans, rinsed and drained
- 1 (15-ounce) can diced tomatoes, undrained
- 2 tablespoons chopped parsley *or* 2 teaspoons dried parsley

In a large pot, heat oil over medium heat. Sauté onion, carrots, celery, and garlic 5–10 minutes, stirring often.

Add remaining ingredients

Season to your liking. Use ginger and cinnamon for an Indian flavor, or try italian seasoning, chili powder, and dried oregano for a spicier version.

Simmer 30–60 minutes, or until desired consistency is reached.

Adjust seasonings to your taste. Serve topped with grated cheese or sesame seeds if desired.

Bean Vegetable Soup with Farro

Farro adds a nutty, crunchy texture and fiber to this nutritious soup

Makes 8 delicious servings

- 2 tablespoons of oil of choice
- 1 cup sliced celery
- 1 cup sliced carrots
- 1 cup chopped onion
- 3 garlic cloves, chopped
- 2 cups chopped kale
- 1 cup halved and sliced zucchini
- 1 cup sweet potato or yam cut into large chunks
- 8 cups chicken or vegetable broth or stock
- 1 1/2 cups white beans (any type) cooked from dried *or* canned white beans, rinsed and drained
- 1/2 teaspoon dried oregano
- 1/2 teaspoon dried thyme
- 3 cups cooked farro
- 1/2 cup chopped parsley

In a large pot, heat oil over medium heat. Add celery, carrots, onion, and garlic. Cook approximately 10 minutes, or until tender.

Add kale, sweet potato or yam, and zucchini. Cook another 10 minutes.

Add the broth or stock, beans, oregano, and thyme. Bring to a boil. Reduce heat and simmer, covered, 30–40 minutes.

Add cooked faro and parsley and simmer 10 minutes longer.

Season with salt, pepper, and additional seasonings of your choice if desired.

Best Black Bean Soup Ever

This soup is high in protein and fiber! Recipe freezes well.

Makes 4-6 servings

- 1 tablespoon oil of choice
- 1 cup chopped onion (white, yellow, or red)
- 1 cup chopped carrots
- 1 cup chopped celery
- 1/2 cup chopped bell pepper, any color (optional)
- 1 potato of choice, peeled and chopped (optional)
- 3 cloves garlic, chopped
- 4–5 cups chicken or vegetable broth or stock
- 2 tablespoons unsweetened cocoa powder
- 1 teaspoon apple cider vinegar or balsamic vinegar
- 1 teaspoon ground cumin
- 1 teaspoon paprika
- 1 teaspoon dried oregano
- 1 teaspoon sugar
- salt and pepper to taste

2 cups black beans (approximately 1 cup dried, soaked and cooked) *or* 2 cups canned black beans, rinsed and drained

small amount of lime zest (optional)

Put oil in medium-sized saucepan. Add onion, garlic, carrots, and celery. Add pepper and potato, if using. Sauté on low approximately 10 minutes, or until slightly brown.

Add broth or stock, cocoa powder, vinegar, cumin, paprika, oregano, sugar, salt, and pepper. Stir well.

Stir in beans and add lime zest, if using. Bring to a boil and simmer, covered, approximately 60 minutes.

Ladle into bowls and enjoy!

Suggested garnishes: sour cream, plain yogurt, shredded cheese, grated parmesan cheese, chopped tomatoes, chopped parsley, or cilantro.

Cabbage Soup Peasant Style

Cabbage is a superfood. The red and green combination in this recipe is sure to please.

Makes 6 hearty servings

- 1 tablespoon oil of choice
- 1 cup sliced celery
- 1 cup chopped white or yellow onion
- 1 cup sliced carrots
- 1 cup diced green or red pepper (optional)
- 1 cup chopped leeks (optional)
- 3 cloves garlic, chopped
- 3 cups coarsely chopped red cabbage
- 3 cups coarsely chopped green cabbage
- 1 beet, peeled and cut into cubes (optional; gives the soup a rich red color and yummy taste)
- 1 (14-ounce) can diced tomatoes, undrained
- 4 cups chicken broth or stock
- 1 teaspoon dried oregano
- 1 teaspoon dried basil
- 1/2 teaspoon salt
- a few dashes of black pepper
- a few dashes of red pepper flakes (optional)

Heat oil in a large pot over medium heat. Add onion, celery, carrots, and garlic, as well as bell pepper and leeks, if using. Sauté until slightly tender.

Stir in cabbage and beet and sauté 10 minutes.

Add tomatoes and chicken broth or stock. Bring to a boil and reduce heat.

Add remaining ingredients. Simmer covered until the cabbage is tender or to your liking. The longer it cooks the better the flavors blend.

Variation: add some sliced sausage, chicken, or beef for a different taste and heartier soup.

Cauliflower-Broccoli Soup

This delicious soup is nourishing and full of healthy fiber.

Makes 6–8 servings

5 cups or less chicken stock or broth, depending on thickness desired
3 cups coarsely chopped broccoli florets, fresh or frozen
3 cups coarsely chopped cauliflower florets, fresh or frozen
1 cup chopped onion
1 cup chopped carrots
1/2 cup chopped celery

4–5 cloves garlic, chopped
1 tablespoon Braggs Liquid Aminos *or* soy sauce
1 teaspoon curry powder
1 teaspoon garlic powder
1/2 teaspoon paprika
dash of cayenne (optional)
salt and pepper (optional)
cheese, grated, for garnish

Slow Cooker Method

Place all ingredients except cheese in a slow cooker sprayed with cooking spray and stir. Cook on low 8–10 hours or on high 5 hours.

When ingredients are tender, slightly mash with masher or immersion blender to desired texture. For a smoother soup, puree in a food processor. (I leave it chunky.)

Garnish individual portions with grated cheese.

Stove Top Method

Sauté all ingredients except broth and cheese in a large pot until slightly tender. Add stock or broth and simmer over low heat 1–2 hours, or until desired consistency is reached.

When ingredients are tender, slightly mash with masher or immersion blender to desired texture. For a smoother soup, puree in a food processor.

Garnish individual portions with grated cheese.

Green Split Pea Soup via
Slow Cooker or Stove

Hearty soup full of fiber and nutrients. Freezes well.

Makes 8 servings

7–8 cups chicken broth or stock *or* a combination of broth or stock and water
2 cups dried split peas, rinsed
1 cup chopped celery
1 cup chopped carrots
1 cup chopped onion
1 large baking potato, peeled and cut into chunks (approximately 1 cup)
1 leek, rinsed and chopped (optional)
1/2 cup chopped turnip (optional)
4 cloves garlic, minced
2 bay leaves
1/2 teaspoon dried thyme leaf
1/2 teaspoon dried marjoram
1 teaspoon dried oregano
1/2 teaspoon salt
pepper to taste
chopped parsley or cilantro for topping (optional)

Slow Cooker Method

Place all ingredients in slow cooker and stir to combine. Cook on low for 8–10 hours. Remove bay leaves. If soup is too thick or dry, thin with more liquid.

Serve as is, or for a creamier texture, mash or puree as desired. Top with parsley or cilantro, if using.

Stove Top Method

In a large pot, lightly sauté all ingredients except peas and liquid for a few minutes.

Add peas and liquid and bring to a boil. Cover and reduce the heat. Simmer 1 hour or more, stirring occasionally, until peas are cooked and desired texture is reached. If soup is too thick or dry, thin with more liquid.

Serve as is, or for a creamier texture, mash or puree as desired. Top with parsley or cilantro, if using.

Variations: Instead of baking potato, substitute some cooked barley, cooked or canned garbanzo beans, diced tomatoes and cumin, or sweet potatoes cut into 1/2-inch cubes.

Healthy Beet-Cabbage Soup

Beets contain a wealth of fiber, half soluble and half insoluble. Both types of fiber help in fighting fat. Cabbage, a cruciferous vegetable, helps detoxify the body. Cabbage is a dieter's friend as it has the fewest calories and least fat of any vegetable, as well as being rich in fiber and vitamin C.

Makes 6–8 servings

1–2 tablespoons oil of choice
3 cups cabbage, largely shredded, use green or red or a combination of each
1 cup chopped, onion, white or yellow
1/2 cup chopped celery
3 cloves of garlic, minced
4 cups chicken or vegetable stock or broth
2 cups water
3–4 large beets, without tops, approximately 1 pound, peeled and largely shredded
1 cup sliced carrots
1 cup potato cubed approximately 1/2 pound (use white, purple or red)1 (14-ounce) can diced tomatoes, undrained or 2 cups chopped fresh tomatoes
1 tablespoon red wine vinegar or lemon juice
1 bay leaf
1/2 teaspoon powdered ginger
1/2 teaspoon salt if desired
small amount of cinnamon, nutmeg, and cloves for more flavor if desired
1/2 cup parsley or dill chopped
2 cups coarsely chopped leafy greens, such as beet or chard (optional)
1 (15-ounce) can white beans, drained and rinsed or 1 1/2 cups cooked from dried (optional)

Heat oil in a large pot . Add cabbage, onions, celery, and garlic. Sauté 10 minutes, or until softened.

Add beets, carrots, potatoes, and liquid. Bring to a boil.

Reduce heat and simmer partially covered 60 minutes, or until potatoes are tender.

Stir in the parsley or dill and greens (if using). Simmer a while longer. Stir in beans, if using. Adjust seasonings if necessary.

Serve warm or cold. Top with sour cream, yogurt, chopped scallions, or more chopped parsley if desired.

Heavenly Butternut Squash Soup

Tastes and looks like heaven in a bowl.

Makes 4-6 servings

1 tablespoon oil of choice
2 cups chopped onion
1/2 cup diced carrots
1/2 cup diced celery
1/2 teaspoon ground nutmeg
1/2 teaspoon ground ginger
2 1/2–3 pounds butternut squash peeled, seeded, and cut into 1-inch pieces (approximately 5–6 cups)
4 cups water *or* 4 cups vegetable or chicken broth or stock for a richer taste

Heat oil in a large pot over medium-high heat. Add onion, celery, carrots, nutmeg, and ginger. Cook over low heat stirring occasionally until mixture is softened, approximately 10 minutes.

Add squash and sauté over low heat another 5–10 minutes, stirring occasionally.

Add water, broth, or stock. Bring to a boil and simmer covered 30–40 minutes, or until vegetables are very tender.

Blend with an immersion blender, food processer, blender, or masher until creamy. Add some additional liquid if soup is too thick.

This soup is delicious plain, but you can serve the soup topped with chopped scallions, parsley or cilantro, or a dollop of yogurt or sour cream if desired.

Soup will keep a few days in the refrigerator, and it freezes well.

Variations: For a different twist, add some diced unpeeled apple, unpeeled pear, or sweet potato when sautéing the squash. You may also add some canned or cooked black beans or cooked farro.

Minestrone Soup a la Linda

With this recipe, you can choose to add some or all of the vegetables listed below for a hearty, healthy, fiber-rich soup.

Makes approximately 8 servings

- 2 tablespoons oil of choice (can use less if desired)
- 3 cups chopped red cabbage
- 1 cup chopped yellow or red onion
- 1 cup sliced carrots
- 1 cup sliced celery
- 4 cloves of garlic, chopped
- 1 cup sliced zucchini or yellow squash
- 1 cup chopped bell pepper (optional)
- 2 tablespoons red wine vinegar or balsamic vinegar
- 2 teaspoons dried basil
- 1 teaspoon dried oregano
- 1/2 teaspoon dried dill
- 1/2 teaspoon cayenne pepper or to taste
- 4 cups chicken broth or stock
- 4 cups water
- 1 (14.5-ounce) can diced tomatoes, undrained
- 1 cup chopped kale, any variety, tough stems removed
- 1/4 cup minced fresh parsley *or* 2 teaspoons dried parsley
- 1 cup of canned beans of your choice, rinsed and drained *or* 1 cup cooked dried beans
- 1/2 cup fiber-rich pasta of choice, uncooked
- 1 cup chopped cauliflower (optional)
- 1 cup green beans, fresh or frozen, cut into desired lengths (optional)
- 1 cup diced red potato, peeled or unpeeled (optional)

- additional seasonings as desired
- grated cheese for topping (optional)

In a large pot, heat oil over medium heat. Add cabbage, onions, carrots, celery, and garlic and cook 10 minutes, stirring often.

Add zucchini or yellow squash, bell pepper (if desired), vinegar, herbs, and cayenne pepper. Cook another 10 minutes.

Add the broth or stock, water, tomatoes, kale and parsley. Bring mixture to a boil. Cover and let simmer 30 minutes.

Add beans, pasta, and remaining vegetables you are using. Simmer covered until the pasta is al dente and the vegetables are tender.

Top with grated cheese if desired. Serve with crusty bread, and relish the flavors.

Red Lentil Soup

This is a meal in a bowl, perfect for a cold night or for when a nourishing comfort food is required. The lentils make it rich in soluble fiber. It freezes well.

Makes 8 or more servings

- 7 cups chicken or vegetable broth or stock *or* use half broth or stock and half water
- 1 (14.5-ounce) can diced tomatoes, undrained
- 1 cup dry red split lentils, rinsed well
- 1 cup sliced carrots
- 1 cup chopped onion
- 1 cup chopped celery
- 1/2 cup uncooked brown rice or barley, rinsed
- 1 tablespoon chopped garlic or an equivalent amount of garlic powder
- 1/2 teaspoon dried basil
- 1/2 teaspoon dried oregano
- 1/2 teaspoon dried thyme leaf
- 1/4 teaspoon ground cumin
- 1 bay leaf
- 1 teaspoon balsamic vinegar (optional)
- additional seasonings to taste (optional)
- 1/3 cup chopped parsley
- plain yogurt for topping

Slow Cooker Method

Assemble all of the ingredients in a 4–6 quart slow cooker. Cook on low 10–12 hours or on high 5–6 hours.

Stir in parsley and serve topped with plain yogurt.

Stovetop Method

Lightly sauté vegetables and herbs in a little oil of choice. Add liquids, lentils, and rice or barley and simmer, covered, 1 hour or more until desired consistency is reached.

Stir in parsley and serve topped with plain yogurt.

Sweet Potato Soup

Warming and nourishing! Sweet potatoes are a good source of fiber and protein; thus they help with blood sugar regulation, providing a steady supply of energy. It's better to leave the skin on whenever eating sweet potatoes, or else you will lose some of the vitamin A, potassium, and protein.

Makes 6 servings

- cooking spray
- 1 tablespoon oil of choice
- 3 cups sweet potatoes cut into 1-inch cubes, scrubbed if organic or peeled if not organic

- 1 cup coarsely chopped onion
- 1 teaspoon minced garlic
- 1 teaspoon ground cumin
- 1 teaspoon ground ginger
- 1 teaspoon orange zest
- 4 cups chicken or vegetable broth or stock
- salt and pepper to taste
- 2 tablespoons parsley or cilantro chopped
- 1/2 cup plain yogurt or plain greek yogurt, plus more for garnish
- pumpkin seeds or sesame seeds for topping

Spray medium size pot with cooking spray. Add oil and sauté sweet potatoes, onions, garlic, cumin, ginger, and orange zest 5–10 minutes.

Add broth or stock and bring to a boil. Reduce heat and simmer covered 45–60 minutes.

Add yogurt. Puree using a blender, immersion blender, food processor, or masher, leaving some sweet potato chunks for texture.

Add salt and pepper to taste. Stir in parsley or cilantro.

Serve topped with more dollops of yogurt and sprinkle with pumpkin or sesame seeds.

White Bean and Kale Soup

Hearty, delicious, fiber-packed soup.

Makes approximately 10 servings

- 1 tablespoon oil of choice
- 2 cups (approximately 8 ounces) kale or swiss chard, washed, stems removed, and coarsely chopped
- 1 cup diced onion, white or yellow
- 1 cup sliced carrots
- 3/4 cup thinly sliced celery
- 3 garlic cloves, minced
- 6–7 cups water; broth or stock of your choice; or half water, half broth or stock (broth or stock makes a richer soup)
- 2 bay leaves
- 2 tablespoons Bragg Liquid Aminos or soy sauce (optional)
- 1/2 teaspoon dried thyme leaf
- 1/2 teaspoon dried rosemary (optional)
- 1/4 teaspoon garlic powder
- 1/4 teaspoon crushed red pepper (optional)
- 2 cups canned small white beans, drained and rinsed *or* small white beans cooked from dried
- 2 tablespoons fresh parsley or cilantro
- 2 cups diced canned tomatoes, drained *or* diced fresh tomatoes (optional)
- 1 medium potato, peeled (or unpeeled, if organic) and diced (optional)
- grated cheese for topping if desired

Sauté kale or swiss chard, onion, celery, carrot, and garlic in oil over low heat until softened, approximately 10–15 minutes.

Add liquid, bay leaves, Bragg Liquid Aminos or soy sauce (if using), and seasonings. Bring to a boil.

Reduce heat, cover, and simmer until vegetables are tender.

Stir in beans and parsley or cilantro, as well as tomatoes and potato, if using. Simmer another 10 minutes.

Remove bay leaves before serving. Try not to overcook.

Yellow Split Pea Soup via
Slow Cooker or Stove

Delicious, fiber-rich pea soup of a different color

Makes 6–8 servings

- 2 tablespoons oil of choice (if using the stove top method)
- 2 cups yellow split peas, rinsed and drained
- 1 cup chopped celery
- 1 cup chopped carrots
- 1 cup chopped red onion
- 1 cup coarsely chopped raw cauliflower
- 4–5 cloves garlic, chopped
- 1 tablespoon ground cumin
- 2 bay leaves *or* some dried basil
- salt and pepper to taste
- dash of cayenne pepper
- additional seasonings as desired
- 6–7 cups chicken broth or stock *or* use part water (adding more liquid if soup needs thinning)
- plain yogurt, paprika, cilantro, or parsley for garnish (optional)

Slow Cooker Method

Assemble all ingredients in a slow cooker. Cook on low 9–10 hours or on high 5–6 hours, or until vegetables are tender. Remove the bay leaves.

Stir well. Serve chunky, or for a smoother texture, blend with an immersion blender, masher, or food processor.

Stove Top Method

In a large pot over medium heat, sauté all ingredients except liquid and split peas in oil for a few minutes.

Add liquid and split peas. Bring to a boil. Cover, reduce heat and simmer for 1 hour or more until desired texture is reached.

Stir well. Serve chunky, or for a smoother texture, blend with an immersion blender, masher, or food processor.

Variation: Add some diced tomatoes, canned or fresh, for a different twist.

Appetizers

Artichoke Spinach Dip

This dip is low in fat and rich in fiber. Make it ahead for the flavors to blend.

Makes 3 cups dip

- small amount of oil of choice or cooking spray
- 1 large onion, chopped (approximately 1 1/2 cups)
- 1 (10-ounce) package frozen chopped spinach, thawed and squeezed dry
- 6 garlic cloves, minced
- 1 teaspoon dried oregano
- 1 teaspoon dried thyme
- 1 teaspoon salt, or to taste
- 1 (15-ounce) can white beans, drained and rinsed (I used cannellini)
- 1 (15-ounce) can water-packed artichoke hearts, drained and coarsely chopped

Sauté onion, spinach, garlic, oregano, thyme and salt in oil or cooking spray in a medium size pan over low heat until tender. Let cool slightly.

Puree beans in a food processor. Add spinach and onion mixture and puree a little more.

Pour mixture into a bowl and gently stir in artichoke hearts. For a creamier dip, add a small amount of plain yogurt.

Chill before serving. Serve with pita chips, cut up veggies, or whatever you like.

Bean Dip

Fiber-rich appetizer or snack. Great for a party or gathering.

Serves 4 or more

- 1/2 tablespoon oil of choice
- 1/3 cup chopped onion or scallions
- 1 garlic clove, chopped
- 1 1/2 cups refried beans, canned or made from scratch (recipe follows) *or* canned beans, rinsed, drained, and mashed
- 1/2 cup or less liquid saved from cooking the beans, liquid saved from the can, or water
- 1/2 teaspoon chili powder
- 1/2 teaspoon paprika
- 1/4 teaspoon ground cumin
- dash of cayenne pepper
- salt to taste
- 1/2 cup chopped fresh tomatoes
- 2 tablespoons plain yogurt or plain greek yogurt
- 1/4 cup chopped parsley or cilantro for garnish
- lime or lemon juice (optional)

In a saucepan over low heat, sauté onions or scallions and garlic in oil until soft and tender.

Add beans, spices, and additional liquid, if necessary. Mix well, mashing more if necessary.

Add tomatoes and yogurt, as well as lemon or lime juice, if desired. Mix well. For a creamier consistency, may be processed in a food processor.

To serve warm, cook until the mixture is bubbling. Garnish with chopped parsley or cilantro.

To serve cold, refrigerate, garnishing the mixture with parsley or cilantro after it has cooled.

Serve with vegetables, chips, pita bread cut into triangles, crackers, pretzels, or whatever you like.

Refried Beans

Yields 3 cups simmered beans

- 1 cup dried pinto, pink, or black beans
- 1 tablespoon oil of choice
- 2 garlic cloves, finely chopped

Soak dried beans in 4 cups of water at least 8 hours or overnight. Or for a quicker soak, you may cover the beans with water in a large pot and bring to a boil; cover and let soak 1–4 hours at room temperature.

Drain and rinse the beans. Place beans and 8 cups fresh water in a pot. Bring to a boil. Reduce heat and simmer 1–1 1/2 hours with the lid slightly ajar until beans are tender. Drain, reserving 1 cup liquid. At this point, beans may be stored up to 3 days, saving some of the cooking liquid in a separate container.

To make the refried beans, heat the oil in a skillet over medium heat. Add garlic and cook a few minutes. Stir in 2 1/2 cups simmered beans with a small amount of reserved cooking liquid or water and cook for 5 minutes.

Continue cooking and stirring, mashing the beans lightly until the mixture resembles a thick paste. Add more liquid if necessary; don't make it too dry. Can use an immersion blender or food processor.

Add additional seasonings to taste.

Serve refried beans immediately or store in the refrigerator. Use to make bean dip, enchiladas, tostadas, burritos, huevos rancheros, and more. Be creative.

Garbanzo Bean–Spinach Dip

Yummy fiber-rich dip.

Yields 2 cups

- 1 cup canned garbanzo beans, rinsed and drained *or* garbanzo beans cooked from dried
- 1/2 cup frozen chopped spinach, thawed and squeezed dry *or* 1 cup dry fresh baby spinach leaves
- 2 cloves garlic
- 1 tablespoon sunflower seeds
- 1 tablespoon lemon juice
- 1 teaspoon oil of choice
- 1/2 teaspoon dehydrated onion flakes
- 1/4 teaspoon paprika
- salt and pepper to taste

Mix all ingredients in food processor until achieving desired texture. A small amount of plain yogurt may be added in after mixing in food processor if extra creaminess is desired.

Serve with vegetables, chips, crackers, or whatever you like.

Red Lentil Dip

Tasty fiber-rich dip of an unusual color.

Makes 3 or more servings

- 1 cup water
- 1/3 cup red lentils, rinsed and drained
- 2 tablespoons chopped onion
- 1 teaspoon lemon juice
- 2 teaspoons ground cumin
- 2 cloves garlic, finely chopped
- salt and pepper to taste
- dash of cayenne and other seasonings (optional)
- 2 or more tablespoons plain yogurt or plain greek yogurt for creaminess
- chopped parsley or cilantro for garnish

Cook lentils and onion in water until tender and liquid is almost gone, approximately 30 minutes. Drain off any remaining liquid.

Mash, blend, or puree lentil-onion mixture. Add remaining ingredients, mixing well.

Garnish with chopped parsley or cilantro. Serve at room temperature with veggies, chips, crackers, or whatever you like.

Roasted Garbanzo Beans (Chickpeas)

Makes a great fiber-rich snack or appetizer!

- 1 (15-ounce) can garbanzo beans, drained and rinsed
- 1–2 tablespoons oil of choice
- salt
- seasonings of choice, such as cayenne pepper, black pepper, dried basil, dried oregano, garlic powder, paprika, cumin, onion powder, cinnamon, or a spice blend you like
- grated parmesan cheese (optional)

Preheat oven to 400 degrees F.

Spread beans out on a paper towel. Dry them and roll them around with the paper towel to remove their thin skins. Discard the skin

In a large bowl, toss beans with salt, seasonings, oil, and parmesan cheese, if using, until well coated.

Spread beans in a single layer on a parchment-lined baking sheet.

Roast until brown and crunchy, about 20–30 minutes. Shake pan halfway through to ensure beans cook evenly. Make sure they don't burn.

Let cool and devour.

Store in an airtight container for up to a week.

Chips/Crisps

There are many vegetables and fruits that can be easily turned into healthy, tasty, fiber-rich chips. Eat and enjoy! These are a great, nutritious snack. Recipes are given for potatoes, beets, apples, kohlrabi, chard, brussels sprouts, kale, and eggplant. Use the vegetable you like best, or experiment and try new veggies.

Baked Potato Chips

Potatoes contain significant amounts of fiber, which helps lower cholesterol in the blood, thereby, decreasing the risk of heart disease.

- 2 large baking potatoes or red potatoes, peeled or unpeeled
- 3 cups near boiling water
- small amount of oil of choice
- suggested seasonings: salt, garlic salt, lemon pepper, garlic powder, paprika, cayenne, or a combination

Preheat oven to 400–450 degrees F.

Scrub potatoes well and slice crosswise into very thin slices using a mandolin, sharp knife or food processor

Place potato slices in a large bowl with the near boiling water. Let stand 10 minutes. Drain and pat dry with paper towels. Soaking potato slices in hot water speeds up the cooking process and results in crispier chips.

Place potato slices in a large bowl. Toss well with some oil and desired seasonings to coat thoroughly.

Arrange potato slices in a single layer on a large, rimmed baking sheet lined with parchment paper or foil, trying not to overlap slices. You may need to use more than one baking sheet, depending on the amount of potato slices you have.

Bake 15–20 minutes until potatoes are browned and crisp. Watch carefully and remove individual chips that brown more quickly than others.

Luscious Beet Chips

Beets contain both types of fiber; this can help fight fat. They also flush out body toxins.

- 2 large fresh beets
- small amount of oil of choice
- sea salt and other spices (cayenne, garlic powder, etc.) to taste

Preheat oven to 350–375 degrees F.

Slice beets into 1/16-inch-thick rounds

Place beet slices in a large bowl. Toss with oil and seasonings to coat thoroughly.

Arrange beet slices in a single layer on large, rimmed baking sheets lined with parchment paper or foil, trying not to overlap the slices. It may be necessary to bake in several batches.

Bake uncovered until edges begin to brown and beets no longer bend, approximately 20 minutes. Turn chips over and bake approximately 10–20 minutes more until beets crisp and dry out. Transfer to wire racks or paper towels. Chips will continue to crisp as they cool.

May be stored in an airtight container at room temperature.

Kohlrabi Chips

Kohlrabi is rich in dietary fiber and vitamins and has no cholesterol.

- 1–2 Kohlrabi bulbs, peeled or unpeeled, ends trimmed and washed
- small amount of oil of choice
- sea salt and pepper

Preheat oven to 350–375 degrees F.

Slice Kohlrabi. Slice thin for crisp texture or more thickly for chewy texture.

Place Kohlrabi slices in a large bowl. Toss with oil and seasonings to coat thoroughly.

Arrange Kohlrabi slices in a single layer on large, rimmed baking sheets lined with parchment paper or foil, trying not to overlap the slices.

Bake 15–20 minutes. Turn chips over and cook another 5–10 minutes until slices are nicely browned and resemble potato chips. Remove chips as they brown.

Add more salt if needed. Chips will continue to crisp as they dry.

Baked Apple Chips

Apples are full of the soluble fiber pectin.

- 2 unpeeled apples, washed, cored, and thinly sliced
- ground cinnamon to taste

Preheat oven to 275 degrees F.

Spread out apples slices in a single layer on large, rimmed baking sheets lined with parchment paper. Sprinkle lightly with the cinnamon

Bake until apples are crisp and edges curl, flipping once, approximately 45 minutes–1 hour. Turn off the oven and let slices cool in the oven about an hour before removing.

Chard Chips

Chard is full of vitamins, minerals, and antioxidants due to its high fiber content. Research suggests that eating chard regularly may lower both cholesterol and blood sugar. The most common varieties are rainbow, green, and swiss; they all have similar flavors. Chard stems can be sliced thin like celery and used in soups or stir fries. Spinach chips can be made the same way as chard.

- 1 bunch chard
- small amount of oil mixed with water
- salt and pepper to taste
- seasonings of choice

Preheat oven to 400 degrees F.

Wash and dry chard leaves. Remove stems. Tear or cut leaves into pieces.

In a large bowl toss leaves with oil-water mixture, salt, pepper, and other seasonings to coat them lightly.

Place leaves in a single layer on foil- or parchment-lined baking sheets. Don't overpack chard on the baking sheet or it will steam and take longer to crisp.

Bake approximately 5–7 minutes, or until leaves reach desired crispness. Alternatively, chips may be baked 50 minutes at 225 degrees F.

Variation: for a different taste, use a splash of balsamic vinegar at the end of baking.

Brussels Sprouts Chips

Brussels sprouts are a good source of dietary fiber as well as protein, iron, and potassium.

- brussels sprouts, washed and dried
- small amount of oil
- salt and pepper to taste
- seasonings of choice

Preheat oven to 400 degrees F.

Separate individual leaves of brussels sprouts. (Broccoli plant leaves can be prepared in the same way.) In a bowl, toss leaves with enough oil to coat lightly. Add salt, pepper, and other seasonings, tossing well

Place leaves in a single layer on foil- or parchment-lined baking sheets.

Bake 5 minutes, or until chips reach desired crispness.

Kale Chips

Kale is a fiber-rich superfood. Some studies have suggested that eating cruciferous vegetables like kale can slow age-related cognitive decline. Kale comes in several varieties, including lacinato, curly, and red Russian.

- 1 bunch of kale
- small amount of oil mixed with water
- seasonings of choice

Preheat oven to 350 degrees F.

Wash and dry kale leaves (a salad spinner works well). Cut away the tough stems. Cut leaves into pieces

Toss leaves with oil-water mixture until lightly coated. Sprinkle on seasonings of choice, tossing well.

Place leaves in a single layer on foil- or parchment-lined baking sheets.

Bake 10 minutes. Rotate pan, gently stir the kale and bake approximately 15 minutes more until chips crisp and edges brown but not burn.

Serve immediately, as chips will lose crispness quickly.

Eggplant Chips

Eggplant is low in calories, and its high fiber content can help keep you feeling full longer.

- 1 medium eggplant, peeled if desired and sliced thin (globe or Japanese work well)
- 1–2 tablespoons oil of choice
- seasonings of choice, such as garlic powder and sea salt

Preheat oven to 400 degrees F.

In a large bowl, toss eggplant slices with oil and seasonings of choice.

Arrange eggplant slices on foil- or parchment-lined baking sheets.

Bake approximately 20 minutes. Turn chips over and bake an additional 12–20 minutes until crispy and brown. If chips are still soft, bake another 3–5 minutes until they reach desired crispness.

Delicious with dip, such as garlic basil.

Fiber-Rich, Guilt-Free
Fries or Wedges

There are several fiber-rich vegetables that can be made into healthier versions of french fries. They are still crispy, crunchy, and satisfying. Recipes are given for potatoes, butternut squash, sweet potatoes or yams, parsnips and turnips.

Potato Wedges

- 2 large baking potatoes cut into 1/2-inch-wide wedges
- small amount of oil of choice
- small amount of water
- seasonings of choice, such as salt, pepper, paprika, or cayenne

Preheat oven to 425 degrees F.

In a bowl, combine wedges, oil, seasonings, and water and toss to coat well. Alternatively, ingredients may be placed in a plastic bag and shaken.

Place wedges in a single layer on parchment-lined baking sheets.

Bake approximately 25–30 minutes until crisp and brown, turning once or twice.

Butternut Squash Fries or Wedges

Butternut squash is a fiber hero, and it's wonderfully delicious!

- 1 butternut squash, peeled, seeded, and cut into wedges or fries; discard seeds
- small amount of oil of choice
- seasonings of choice, such as salt, pepper, paprika, cumin, cinnamon, coriander, or chili powder

Preheat oven to 400 degrees F.

Place all ingredients in a large bowl and toss well or place the ingredients in a plastic bag and shake well.

Arrange squash in a single layer on parchment-lined baking sheets

Bake approximately 45 minutes, or until the inside of fries or wedges is tender and outside is golden brown. Turn once while baking.

Sweet Potato or Yam Fries or Wedges

These are delicious for a fiber-rich and guilt free snack; they can also be cut into chips.

Serves 4 or more

- 1 pound (approximately 4 medium) sweet potatoes or yams, peeled or unpeeled
- 2 tablespoons or less of oil of choice
- salt and pepper to taste
- seasonings of choice, such as garlic powder, chili powder, cumin, or curry

Preheat oven to 400 degrees F.

Lightly coat rimmed baking sheets with cooking spray or line with foil or parchment paper.

Cut sweet potatoes or yams lengthwise into strips, wedges, or chips.

In a large bowl, toss sweet potatoes or yams with the oil and seasonings or place the ingredients in a plastic bag and shake well.

Lay sweet potatoes or yams in a single layer on prepared baking sheets.

Bake approximately 15 minutes. Turn over and bake 10–15 minutes more until golden brown. If not yet crisp, bake 3–5 minutes more, checking carefully to prevent burning.

Enjoy hot or cold. Serve with dip or eat plain.

Turnip Fries or Wedges

Turnips are a great source of minerals and antioxidants. They are high in dietary fiber and low in calories.

- 2–3 pounds smaller turnips, peeled and cut into 1/2 × 3–inch sticks
- small amount of oil of choice
- seasonings of choice, such as garlic salt, paprika, onion powder, or parmesan cheese

Preheat oven to 425 degrees F.

In a large bowl, toss turnips with the oil and seasonings or place the ingredients in a plastic bag and shake well.

Spread turnips in a single layer on foil- or parchment-lined baking sheets

Bake until crisp on the outside, approximately 30 minutes, turning once. These can be broiled a few minutes per side if more crispness is desired.

Parsnip Fries for a Change

Parsnips are rich in several health-benefitting phytonutrients, vitamins, and minerals. They are an excellent source of both soluble and insoluble dietary fiber. Try fries made from parsnips for a change from traditional potato fries.

- 1 pound parsnips, peeled, sliced into thin strips (cut them similar in size for more even baking), and dried
- 1–2 tablespoons oil of choice
- seasonings of choice, such as garlic powder, sea salt, or cayenne pepper

Preheat oven to 450 degrees F.

In a large bowl, toss the parsnip strips with the oil and seasonings or place the ingredients in a plastic bag and shake well.

Place in a single layer on a rimmed baking sheet coated with cooking spray or lined with parchment paper or nonstick foil.

Bake approximately 20 minutes, stirring occasionally, until golden brown.

Enjoy them hot! For a tasty treat, sprinkle fries with grated parmesan cheese.

Salads and Slaws

Apple Slaw

This slaw is tasty and refreshing; it is a great way to use apples during their peak season.

Makes 4 servings

- 3 cups thinly sliced unpeeled tart green apples, sweet red apples, or a combination of both
- 1 tablespoon lemon juice
- 1 1/2 cups shredded red cabbage
- 2/3 cup red or green grapes, sliced in half (use more depending on your taste)
- 1/2 cup thinly sliced celery
- 2 tablespoons olive oil or oil of choice
- 1 tablespoon honey
- 1/2 teaspoon ground ginger
- 1 teaspoon poppy seeds
- 1/4 cup sliced almonds or other chopped nuts (optional)

In a large bowl, toss apples with lemon juice. Stir in the cabbage, grapes, and celery.

In another bowl, mix together olive oil, honey, and ginger to form a dressing.

Pour dressing over apple mixture and toss gently. Add the poppy seeds. Cover and chill 1–24 hours before serving.

If including nuts, add just before serving.

Bok Choy Salad/Slaw

This is a delightful, light salad that accompanies meat, poultry, or fish well. It can also be eaten unaccompanied.

Makes 4 servings

- 5 cups thinly sliced raw bok choy, any type (approximately 1 1/2 pounds)
- 1 tablespoon soy sauce or Bragg Liquid Aminos
- 1 tablespoon rice vinegar
- 1 tablespoon olive oil or oil of choice
- 1 teaspoon sugar

Place bok choy in a large bowl.

In another bowl, mix together soy sauce or Bragg Liquid Aminos, rice vinegar, olive oil, and sugar. Pour over sliced bok choy and stir gently.

Top each individual serving with sesame seeds or chopped nuts, if desired.

Broccoli Slaw

Broccoli is a rich source of both insoluble and soluble fiber; eating broccoli helps to satisfy the need for both types of fiber. This is great as a side dish or light lunch.

Makes 4 servings

- 1 cup broccoli stalks cut into matchsticks (first shave off or peel tough outer part)
- 1/2 cup chopped broccoli florets (optional)
- 1/2 cup carrots cut into matchsticks
- 1/2 cup celery cut into matchsticks
- 1/2 cup shredded red cabbage
- 1/2 cup dried cranberries or dried cherries
- 1/2–1 cup diced apple (optional)
- 1/3 cup chopped red onion
- 2 tablespoons lemon juice
- 2 tablespoons pumpkin seeds
- 1 tablespoon olive oil or oil of choice
- 1 teaspoon honey or maple syrup
- 1 teaspoon yellow mustard
- 1/4 teaspoon garlic powder

Combine all the ingredients in a large bowl. May substitute equivalent amount of broccoli slaw mix for broccoli stalks, carrots, and celery. Toss well.

Cover and chill before serving.

Carrot Slaw

Great way to get your vitamin K and beta-carotene for the day!

Makes 4 servings

- 1 tablespoon lime juice
- 3/4 teaspoon honey
- dash of salt
- 2 tablespoons olive oil or oil of choice
- 2 cups shredded carrots, unpeeled and cleaned well if using organic
- 1 cup diced green apple, unpeeled and cored (approximately 1/4-inch pieces)
- 3 tablespoons chopped parsley

In a small bowl, whisk together lime juice, honey, and salt. Slowly mix in oil until all ingredients are combined well to make the dressing.

In a large bowl, combine carrots, apple, and parsley. Add dressing and mix well.

If making ahead, cover and refrigerate. Use within a couple of days for optimum taste.

Variations:

Add some shredded red cabbage.

Use red wine vinegar instead of lime juice.

Add some ground cumin, black pepper, or both for more spice.

Cooling Green Pea Salad

Peas have antioxidants and anti-inflammatory benefits, as well as fiber and protein. This recipe makes a great side dish.

Makes 4–6 servings

- 8–10 ounces frozen green peas, thawed
- 1/2 cup thinly sliced celery
- 1/2 cup shredded carrots
- 1/2 cup shredded jicama
- 1/2 cup cherry tomatoes, cut into half or quarters if they are large *or* diced larger tomatoes
- 1/4 cup chopped scallions or red onion
- 1/4 cup plain yogurt or plain greek yogurt
- 1 tablespoon unseasoned rice vinegar
- 1 tablespoon chopped fresh basil
- 1 teaspoon honey or maple syrup
- 1/2 teaspoon curry powder
- salt and pepper to taste
- additional seasonings to taste
- sesame seeds or pumpkin seeds for garnish

Mix all ingredients together lightly. Refrigerate before serving. Sprinkle garnish on each individual serving.

Crisp Green Bean Salad

Green beans are a rich source of dietary fiber, have an impressive amount of antioxidants and can provide cardiovascular benefits.

Makes 6 servings

- 1 pound green beans, washed, trimmed, and cut to desired length or left whole
- 1 cup grape or cherry tomatoes, halved
- 2 tablespoons olive oil or oil of choice
- 2 tablespoons diced scallions *or* 1/4 cup diced red onion
- 1 tablespoon balsamic vinegar, red wine vinegar, or lemon juice
- 1/2 teaspoon sugar
- 1/4 teaspoon dry mustard
- 1/4 teaspoon garlic powder
- salt and pepper to taste
- additional seasonings if desired

Steam green beans until still bright green and desired crispness or tenderness is reached. Plunge into an ice bath for a few minutes to stop the cooking process.

Lightly mix all ingredients together and chill at least 1 hour.

Sprinkle with sesame seeds or chopped walnuts before serving. Serve cold.

Raw Brussels Sprouts and Apple Salad

Crunchy and healthy!

Serves 6 or more

- 4–5 cups thinly sliced or shredded raw brussels sprouts
- 1 1/2 cups thinly sliced unpeeled apple
- 1/2 cup chopped nuts, such as almonds or walnuts
- 1/3 cup feta or goat cheese
- 1/3 cup dried cranberries or dried cherries
- 1/3 cup lemon juice
- 3 tablespoons olive oil or oil of choice
- 1 teaspoon garlic powder
- 1/4 teaspoon ground ginger, salt, pepper, and additional seasonings of choice to taste
- plain yogurt or plain greek yogurt to taste

Combine all ingredients except yogurt in a bowl, tossing well.

Add enough yogurt to achieve desired consistency.

Serve immediately or serve chilled.

Red and Green Cabbage-Apple Slaw

This cabbage slaw offers a break from creamy cabbage slaw or salad. Enjoy the crunchy texture of the cabbage and carrots mingled with the crisp apple and tart lemon.

Makes 4–6 servings

- 3 cups or so shredded cabbage, half red and half green
- 1 large green apple, diced (approximately 1 cup)
- 1/2 cup grated carrots
- 1/4 cup chopped scallions
- 1/4 cup grated nuts (I used pecans)
- 2 tablespoons lemon juice or apple cider vinegar
- 1 tablespoon olive oil or oil of choice
- 1 tablespoon honey or maple syrup
- 1 teaspoon dijon mustard
- dashes of salt and pepper
- small amount of raisins, dried cranberries, dried cherries, or other dried fruit (optional)

Mix cabbage and apple in a large bowl. Add remaining ingredients and stir gently.

Refrigerate at least 1 hour before serving to let the flavors meld. Store in refrigerator if not being eaten soon.

Sprinkle with sesame seeds before serving if desired

Refreshing Jicama Slaw

This is a delightful, fresh-tasting slaw.

Makes 4 servings

- 2 cups peeled and shredded jicama
- 1 cup shredded carrots
- 1/2 teaspoon honey or sugar
- 1/4 cup chopped cilantro or chopped parsley
- 1 tablespoon lime juice or unseasoned rice vinegar
- 1 tablespoon olive oil or oil of choice
- 1/4 teaspoon chili powder or to taste
- salt and pepper to taste
- shredded red cabbage, sliced bell pepper, or sliced red onion (optional)
additional seasonings of choice (optional)

Lightly mix together all ingredients in a large bowl. Refrigerate if not eaten immediately.

Sprinkle each individual serving with sesame seeds, if desired. Best if eaten within a day or two.

Salubrious Beet Slaw

Makes a healthy and tangy side dish or first course.

Makes 4 servings

- enough beets to make approximately 1 cup matchstick-sized pieces
- 1/2 cup unpeeled tart green apple (such as Granny Smith or Pippin) sliced into matchstick size pieces
- 1/2 cup chopped parsley or cilantro
- 1/2 cup orange segments, peeled and cut into small pieces (optional)
- 2 tablespoons olive oil or oil of choice
- 2 tablespoons sliced scallions
- 1 tablespoon lemon juice
- 1 tablespoon lemon zest
- 1/2 teaspoon honey
- salt and pepper to taste

Wash, peel, and steam beets until slightly tender. Immediately immerse beets in an ice bath for a few minutes. Cut into matchsticks.

Combine all ingredients in a large bowl and toss gently to coat. Serve immediately or serve chilled. Best if eaten within a few days.

Spinach Salad

Fiber-rich salad with pizzazz.

Makes 4 servings

- 4 cups fresh baby spinach, rinsed and dried
- 2 oranges, peeled and separated into 1-inch segments (approximately 2 cups)
- 1 cup thinly sliced green apple (such as Pippin), unpeeled and cored
- 1/3 cup thinly sliced red onion
- 1/4 cup chopped parsley or cilantro
- 2 tablespoons dried cranberries, tart dried cherries, or raisins
- 1 tablespoon olive oil or oil of choice
- 1 tablespoon balsamic vinegar
- 1 teaspoon yellow mustard
- 1/2 teaspoon sugar or honey
- 1/4 teaspoon grated orange zest
- 1/4 teaspoon dried thyme leaf
- 1/4 teaspoon salt
- 1 cup white beans, cooked from dried *or* canned white beans, rinsed and drained (optional)
- crumbled feta cheese or other cheese (optional)
- additional seasonings of choice (optional)

In a large bowl, toss together spinach, orange segments, apple, onion, parsley or cilantro, and dried fruit.

In a separate bowl, mix together the oil, vinegar, mustard, sugar or honey, orange zest, dried thyme, and salt. Drizzle over the other ingredients and toss gently. If desired, add beans and toss with cheese and other seasonings.

Tangy Red Cabbage-Carrot Slaw

The tangy flavors will revitalize your taste buds.

Makes 4–6 servings

- 4 cups shredded red cabbage (approximately 1 pound)
- 2 cups shredded carrots, unpeeled if organic (approximately 3–4 carrots)
- 1 medium green apple, unpeeled and diced (approximately 1 cup)
- 1/3 cup diced scallions
- 1/2 cup chopped parsley or cilantro
- 1/4 cup lemon juice
- 2 tablespoons olive oil or of choice

- 1 tablespoon apple cider vinegar
- 1 tablespoon honey
- 1/4 teaspoon garlic powder
- salt and pepper to taste

In a large bowl, mix together cabbage, apple, carrots, scallions, and parsley or cilantro.

In a separate bowl, combine remaining ingredients. Drizzle over cabbage-apple mixture and gently combine. Add additional seasonings if desired.

Chill awhile before serving.

Variation: Add some raisins, dried cherries, dried cranberries, or grapes for added sweetness.

Baked Goods

Carrot Blueberry Oat Muffins without Guilt

Makes 12 muffins

- 1 cup white whole wheat flour
- 1 cup old-fashioned oats
- 1/2 cup chopped nuts (I used almonds)
- 2 teaspoons baking powder
- 1 teaspoon baking soda
- 1 teaspoon ground cinnamon
- 1/2 teaspoon ground nutmeg
- 1/4 teaspoon ground cloves
- 1 cup finely shredded carrots, unpeeled if organic
- 1 cup fresh blueberries *or* frozen blueberries, thawed
- 1/2 cup brown sugar
- 1/2 cup fresh orange juice
- 1/2 cup plain nonfat yogurt
- 2 eggs, slightly beaten
- 2 tablespoons oil of choice
- 1 teaspoon orange zest
- 1 teaspoon vanilla extract

Preheat oven to 400 degrees F. Place paper liners in a 12-cup muffin pan.

In a large bowl, mix together dry ingredients.

In a separate bowl, mix carrots, blueberries, brown sugar, orange juice, yogurt, eggs, oil, orange zest, and vanilla extract.

Gently fold wet ingredients into dry ingredients and mix until blended.

Evenly divide batter between muffin cups.

Bake approximately 15 minutes, or until toothpick inserted in center comes out clean. Cool in muffin tin 5 minutes.

Remove from muffin tin. Serve warm if desired.

Devour without any guilt.

Fall for Pear Pumpkin Muffins

Perfect recipe to bake in the fall when the fresh pears are in season. Both the pears and pumpkin provide fiber, as well as other nutrients.

Makes 12 muffins

- 2 teaspoons vinegar or lemon juice
- scant 1/2 cup milk or non-dairy milk of choice
- 2 eggs, slightly beaten
- 1 cup diced fresh pears, unpeeled, preferably organic
- 1/2 cup canned pumpkin *or* pureed cooked fresh pumpkin

- 1/3 cup brown sugar
- 1/4 cup cooking oil of choice
- 2 cups white whole wheat flour
- 1 teaspoon baking powder
- 1/2 teaspoon baking soda
- 1/2 teaspoon ground cinnamon
- 1/4 teaspoon ground nutmeg
- 1/4 teaspoon ground ginger
- 1/2 cup semisweet or dark chocolate chips *or* coarsely ground nuts

Preheat oven to 375 degrees F. Place paper liners in a 12-cup muffin pan.

Place vinegar or lemon juice in 1/2-cup glass measuring cup and add enough milk to make 1/2 cup total liquid. Stir and let mixture stand 5 minutes to sour before using.

Gently mix together the eggs, pears, pumpkin, sugar, oil, and soured milk.

In another bowl, stir together flour, baking powder, baking soda, cinnamon, nutmeg, and ginger. Make a well in center of dry ingredients. Add wet ingredients and mix till moistened. Stir in chocolate chips or nuts.

Divide batter evenly among prepared muffin cups, filling each about 2/3 full.

Bake 20–25 minutes until golden brown and a toothpick inserted in center comes out clean.

Cool in muffin tin 5 minutes. Remove from muffin tin.

Serve warm if desired.

Fudgy Healthy Brownies

Makes 12 brownies

- 2 large eggs
- 3/4 cup brown sugar, preferably dark brown
- 3/4 cup cooked fresh winter squash or frozen, thawed (butternut or acorn works great) or use sweet potato
- 2/3 cup unsweetened cocoa powder
- 1/3 cup whole wheat flour or white whole wheat flour
- 1/3 cup semisweet or bittersweet chocolate chips
- 1/3 cup chopped nuts
- 3 tablespoons oil of choice or use 3 tablespoons applesauce
- 1 teaspoon vanilla extract
- 1/2 teaspoon ground cinnamon

Preheat oven to 350 degrees F. Coat an 8-inch or 9-inch square pan with cooking spray.

Mix all ingredients in a large bowl until combined.

Pour batter into pan and bake 23–25 minutes until brownies are springy to the touch.

Cool and cut into 12 squares.

Dust with confectioners' sugar before serving if desired (not necessary).

Variation: For a different flavor, add 1/4 cup dried cherries.

Kale-Apple Yum Muffins

These yummy muffins are bursting with fiber from the apples, kale, figs, and nuts.

Makes 12 muffins

- 1 1/2 cups white whole wheat flour
- 1 teaspoon baking powder
- 1 teaspoon baking soda
- 1 teaspoon ground cinnamon
- 1/2 teaspoon ground nutmeg
- 1/2 teaspoon salt (optional)
- 1 egg
- 1 1/2 cups grated unpeeled apples, preferably organic
- 1 cup finely chopped kale with the stems removed (can substitute other green leafy vegetables too)
- 1/2 cup chopped dried figs
- 1/2 cup plain yogurt, preferably greek yogurt
- 1/3 cup honey
- 1/4 cup oil of choice
- 1 teaspoon vanilla extract
- 1/3 cup chopped nuts (optional, but gives the muffins more crunch)

Preheat oven to 400 degrees F. Line a 12-cup muffin tin with paper liners.

In a large bowl, combine flour, baking powder, baking soda, cinnamon, nutmeg, and salt.

In a separate bowl, combine egg, apple, kale, figs, yogurt, honey, oil, and vanilla extract, as well as nuts, if using.

Add wet ingredients to dry ingredients, stirring just until moistened.

Fill muffin cups 2/3 full.

Bake 15 minutes, or until a toothpick inserted in center comes out clean or tops spring back when touched.

Cool in muffin tin 5 minutes. Remove from muffin tin

Serve warm if desired

Luscious Lemon Poppy Seed Loaf

1 cup sugar (either white or brown)

1 cup white whole wheat flour

1 cup nonfat plain greek yogurt* or regular nonfat plain yogurt

1/2 cup freshly squeezed lemon juice

1/3 cup poppy seeds

1/4 cup oil of choice

3 large eggs

2 tablespoons fresh lemon zest

1 1/4 teaspoons baking powder

1 teaspoon vanilla extract

3/4 teaspoon baking soda

*Loaf is denser if using greek yogurt instead of regular yogurt

Preheat oven to 350 degrees F. Coat a 9 × 5–inch loaf pan with cooking spray.

Mix all ingredients in a large bowl. Pour batter into pan.

Bake approximately 40 minutes until toothpick inserted in center comes out clean.

Let loaf rest in pan for a while before removing to a cooling rack.

Slice and enjoy!

Orange-Cranberry Muffins

Makes 12 muffins

- 2 cups white whole wheat flour
- 1 tablespoon orange zest
- 2 teaspoons baking powder
- 1 teaspoon ground ginger
- 1/2 teaspoon baking soda
- 1/2 teaspoon salt (optional)
- 1/3 cup brown sugar
- 1 egg, slightly beaten
- 3/4 cup orange juice
- 1/4 cup oil of choice
- 1/2 teaspoon vanilla extract
- 1 cup fresh cranberries, sliced in half
- 1/2 cup chopped nuts

Preheat oven to 350 degrees F. Place paper liners in a 12-cup muffin tin.

In large bowl, combine flour, orange zest, baking powder, baking soda, ginger, and salt, if using.

In another bowl, whisk together brown sugar, egg, orange juice, oil, and vanilla extract. Stir in cranberries and nuts.

Make a well in center of dry ingredients. Add wet ingredients to dry and stir until moistened. Do not overmix. Batter will be lumpy.

Divide batter evenly between muffin cups. Bake approximately 15–20 minutes until lightly browned and toothpick inserted into muffin center comes out clean.

Cool in muffin tin for 5 minutes. Remove from muffin tin. Eat warm if desired.

Pinto Bean Brownies

You will love these fiber-rich brownies with a unique taste!

Makes 16 brownies

- 1 cup pinto beans, cooked from dried *or* canned pinto beans, rinsed and drained
- 2 eggs
- 1/2 cup brown sugar
- 1/2 cup applesauce (I used homemade*, but you can use jarred or canned)
- 1/2 cup bittersweet or semisweet chocolate chips
- 1/3 cup white whole wheat flour
- 1/3 cup unsweetened cocoa powder or raw cacao powder
- 1/3 cup chopped nuts (optional)
- 1/4 cup milk or nondairy milk
- 2 teaspoons vanilla extract
- 3/4 teaspoon baking powder
- 1/4 teaspoon baking soda

Preheat oven to 350 degrees F. Coat an 8-inch or 9-inch square baking pan with cooking spray.

Puree beans with eggs. Pour mixture into a large bowl and mix with remaining ingredients.

Pour batter into prepared pan. Bake 45 minutes, or until toothpick inserted into center comes out clean and center is set. Let cool.

Cut into 16 squares and serve.

*For homemade applesauce: See recipe in Desserts section of cookbook

Sunburst Carrot Loaf

This recipe has a unique blend of fiber-rich ingredients.

- 1 1/2 cups white whole wheat flour
- 1 1/2 cups shredded carrots
- 1 cup diced mango or guava, either fresh or frozen and thawed
- 1 cup chopped kale, stems removed
- 1/2 cup sugar
- 1/2 cup chopped nuts of choice (optional)
- 1/4 cup oil of choice
- 2 eggs slightly beaten
- 1 teaspoon vanilla extract
- 1 teaspoon ground cinnamon
- 1 teaspoon baking soda
- 1/2 teaspoon baking powder
- 1/2 teaspoon ground nutmeg

Preheat oven to 350 degrees F. Coat a 9 × 5–inch loaf pan with cooking spray.

Gently mix all ingredients together until combined.

Pour into loaf pan and bake 40–45 minutes, or until toothpick inserted in center comes out clean.

Cool on a rack in pan 10 minutes, and then gently remove loaf from pan and continue cooling on rack.

Slice and enjoy!

Delectable Pear Loaf

- 2 cups chopped unpeeled pears
- 1 1/2 cups white whole wheat flour
- 3/4 cup plain yogurt (I used greek)
- 3/4 cup brown sugar
- 1/2 cup chocolate pieces (optional)
- 1/2 cup ground nuts (optional)
- 1/4 cup oil of choice
- 2 large eggs
- 1 tablespoon lemon zest
- 1 tablespoon lemon juice
- 1 teaspoon vanilla extract
- 1 teaspoon ground cinnamon
- 1 teaspoon baking powder
- 1/2 teaspoon baking soda
- 1/2 teaspoon ground nutmeg
- 1/4 teaspoon ground ginger

Preheat oven to 350 degrees F. Coat a 9 × 5–inch loaf pan with cooking spray.

Mix all ingredients together in a large bowl.

Pour batter into loaf pan and bake 40 minutes, or until toothpick inserted in center comes out clean.

Cool in pan 10 minutes, and then gently remove loaf from pan. Continue cooling on a rack.

Slice and enjoy!

Snacks and Treats

Chocolatey Oat Treats

Treats full of fiber and antioxidants.

Makes about 4 servings of 2 treats

- 1/4 cup semisweet or bittersweet chocolate chips
- 1/4 cup finely diced dried apricots
- 2 tablespoons creamy peanut butter or creamy almond butter
- 2 tablespoons low fat, nonfat, or non-dairy milk of choice
- 3/4 old-fashioned rolled oats

Mix chocolate chips, apricots, nut butter, and milk in a saucepan, and cook over low heat until chocolate melts, approximately 3 minutes or less.

Stir in oats while mixture is still on stove. Remove from heat and stir until combined.

Using a melon baller, small ice cream scoop, or spoon, drop ball-shaped portions on a baking sheet lined with wax paper, parchment paper, or foil.

Chill balls in refrigerator 10 minutes or longer before serving.

Dark Chocolate Nut Bark

Guiltlessly satisfies those chocolate cravings!

Makes approximately 10 large pieces or numerous smaller pieces

- 7 or more ounces dark chocolate (60–70 percent cocoa solids, preferably)
- nuts, chopped to desired consistency (use whatever nut you like best)

Line a 9 × 13–inch baking sheet or pan with heavy-duty foil or parchment paper and chill in refrigerator 10 minutes or more.

Break chocolate into chunks if necessary and melt in a double boiler over simmering water or in the microwave, stirring carefully so chocolate won't burn.

Spread melted chocolate evenly on chilled pan and shape into a roughly 9 × 13–inch rectangle; the larger the rectangle, the thinner the pieces. Sprinkle chopped nuts evenly over top of chocolate rectangle.

Chill 10 minutes or longer in refrigerator.

Break chocolate rectangle into 3-inch or smaller pieces.

Serve and enjoy.

Fruity Nut Bark

This treat is chock-full of fiber and antioxidants.

Makes approximately 10 large pieces or numerous smaller pieces

- 1/2 cup each dried cherries, dried cranberries, and chopped dried pineapple (or use any combination of chopped dried fruit desired)
- 1/2 cup chopped raw cashews or nuts of choice
- 7 ounces dark chocolate (60–70 percent cocoa solids, preferably)

Line a 9 × 13–inch baking sheet or pan with heavy-duty foil or parchment paper and chill in refrigerator 10 minutes or more.

Combine dried fruit and nuts in a bowl and stir well.

Break chocolate into chunks, if necessary, and melt in a double boiler over simmering water or in the microwave, stirring carefully so chocolate won't burn.

Stir half of fruit-and-nut mixture into melted chocolate. Spread the chocolate mixture evenly over chilled pan and shape into a 9 × 13–inch rectangle. Sprinkle the remaining fruit-and-nut mixture evenly over top of chocolate rectangle.

Chill 10 minutes or longer in refrigerator.

Break chocolate rectangle into 3-inch or smaller pieces.

Serve and enjoy. It won't last long.

Super-Easy Trail Mix

This is a healthy fiber-rich trail mix. It won't last long.

- 1/2 cup coarsely chopped nuts of choice, such as dry roasted peanuts, cashews, almonds, walnuts, or a mixture
- 1/2 cup high-fiber cereal, such as toasted oats, squares, or flakes
- 1/3 cup seeds, such as pumpkin, sunflower, or pine nuts
- 1/4 cup dark or bittersweet chocolate chips
- 1/4 cup dried cherries or dried cranberries
- 1/4 cup raisins
- 1/4 teaspoon chili powder or cayenne (optional)
- 1/4 teaspoon ground cinnamon (optional)
- dash of turmeric (optional)

Toss all ingredients together in a bowl. Mix well.

Store in an airtight container.

Variation: You may use other dried fruits if you like them better.

Desserts

Apple-Cranberry Crisp

Delicious. Everyone loves this one! The cranberries contribute a considerable fiber boost as well as a tart taste. Recipe can be cut in half or doubled. Freezes well.

Makes 10–12 servings

- 3 cups thinly sliced unpeeled apples (approximately 2 large), preferably organic
- 12 ounces fresh cranberries, rinsed
- 1/2 cup sugar
- 1 teaspoon ground cinnamon
- 1/4 teaspoon ground nutmeg
- 4 tablespoons white whole wheat flour or whole wheat flour, divided
- 2 tablespoons brown sugar
- 3/4 cup old-fashioned oats
- 1/2 cup chopped nuts (almonds or walnuts work well)
- 3 tablespoons butter or butter alternative of choice, melted

Coat a 3-quart baking dish with cooking spray. Preheat oven to 350 degrees F.

In a large bowl, combine apples, cranberries, sugar, cinnamon, nutmeg, and 1 tablespoon flour. Mix well. Pour mixture into baking dish.

In the same bowl, combine remaining flour, brown sugar, oats, and nuts. Stir in melted butter or margarine. Mix well. Mixture will be crumbly.

Sprinkle crumble over fruit mixture.

Bake 40 minutes, or until crisp is lightly browned.

Let stand at least 10 minutes before serving. Serve warm or cold.

Bread Pudding

Makes a yummy, fiber-rich breakfast or dessert.

Makes 2–3 servings

- 2 slices whole wheat bread or bread of choice, cut into 1/2-inch cubes (approximately 1 1/2 cups)
- 1/3 cup raisins or currants *or* 1/2 cup diced apple, unpeeled if organic, and 2 tablespoons raisins
- 1 1/4 cups milk or nondairy milk (may need a little more)
- 2 eggs
- 1 teaspoon vanilla extract
- 1 teaspoon ground cinnamon
- dash of ground nutmeg

Preheat oven to 350 degrees F. Coat an 8-inch square casserole dish with cooking spray.

Arrange bread cubes in casserole dish, and sprinkle with fruit.

Combine milk, eggs, vanilla, cinnamon, and nutmeg in a large bowl. Beat mixture until smooth. Pour milk mixture over bread, making sure bread is well moistened.

Bake about 35–40 minutes until pudding is lightly browned and a knife inserted in center comes out clean.

Cool slightly, but serve warm.

Creamy Chia Seed Pudding

Chia seeds are popular today, as they are loaded with antioxidants, protein, omega-3 fatty acids, and fiber. They have a neutral flavor and nutty texture. This pudding is a delicious way to incorporate them into your diet.

Makes 2-3 servings

- 1 cup unsweetened non-dairy milk of choice (I used unsweetened coconut milk, but it tastes great with nut milks)
- 1/4 cup chia seeds
- 2 tablespoons raw cacao powder or unsweetened cocoa powder

- 1 tablespoon honey or maple syrup
- 1 1/2 teaspoons vanilla extract
- 1 teaspoon grated orange zest
- 1/4 teaspoon ground cinnamon
- dash of salt

Mix all ingredients in a bowl. Adjust amount of sweetness and amount of cocoa to your liking. Let mixture sit in refrigerator 2 hours or overnight.

Serve topped with dark chocolate shavings, berries, nuts, bananas, fresh citrus segments, coconut flakes, or toppings of your choosing. Be creative.

Variation: For a more chocolatey taste, add some melted dark chocolate or chocolate chips.

Dark Chocolate Avocado Mousse

Avocados are a naturally nutrient-dense food; they contain heart-healthy compounds, vitamins, and minerals, as well as fiber and protein. Unsweetened cocoa is low in calories and fiber rich; it contains essential minerals that support your heart, bones, and immune system. This mousse is good for you!

Makes 2-3 servings

- 1 small ripe avocado (approximately 1/2 cup)
- 2 tablespoons unsweetened cocoa powder or raw cacao powder
- 2 tablespoons milk or nondairy milk of choice (more if needed to thin the mousse)
- 2 tablespoons plain yogurt, preferably greek yogurt
- 1 tablespoon honey, maple syrup, or sweetener of choice (more if a sweeter taste is desired)
- 1 teaspoon vanilla extract
- 1/4 teaspoon ground cinnamon

Mash avocado in a bowl. Add remaining ingredients and mix well, or mix all ingredients in a blender until smooth.

Chill if desired.

Serve plain or top with chopped nuts, coconut flakes, or a fruit of choice, such as berries. It won't last long!

Variations:

For a coffee flavor, add 1 teaspoon instant coffee.

For a more chocolatey flavor, add some melted dark chocolate or chocolate chips

Divine Peach-Berry Crisp

This crisp is a tasty combination of tantalizing and tasty fruit flavors.

Makes 8 servings

- 2 cups blueberries, boysenberries, or blackberries *or* 1 (16-ounce) package frozen berries, thawed and juices drained
- 3 cups sliced peaches or nectarines (approximately 3 medium), unpeeled if organic *or* 1 (16-ounce) package frozen sliced peaches or nectarines, thawed
- 1/2 cup old-fashioned oats
- 1/3 cup brown sugar
- 1/3 cup white whole wheat flour or regular whole wheat flour
- 2 tablespoons chopped nuts, such as walnuts, almonds, or pecans
- 2 tablespoons oil of choice
- 1 teaspoon ground cinnamon
- 1/2 teaspoon ground nutmeg
- 1/4 teaspoon ground cloves

Preheat oven to 350 degrees F. Coat an 8-inch square pan with cooking spray.

Layer fruit in pan. Lightly mix together remaining ingredients in a bowl. Sprinkle over fruit.

Bake approximately 30 minutes, or until golden.

Serve warm or cold. Delicious topped with ice cream.

Pear Crisp

Absolutely scrumptious! Perfect recipe for fresh pear season.

Makes 6 yummy servings

Filling:

- 4 cups thinly sliced firm, ripe, unpeeled pears, preferably organic
- 1 tablespoon grated lemon zest
- 1 tablespoon lemon juice
- 1/2 cup brown sugar

- 1/2 cup old-fashioned oats
- 1/3 cup chopped nuts (walnuts, almonds, pecans, etc.)
- 1/3 cup white whole wheat flour or whole wheat flour
- 1/4 cup oil of choice
- 1 1/4 teaspoons ground cinnamon
- 3/4 teaspoon ground nutmeg

Preheat oven to 375 degrees F. Coat an 8-inch or 9-inch square pan with cooking spray.

Mix pears, lemon zest, and lemon juice and spread over bottom of prepared dish.

Lightly mix remaining ingredients in a medium bowl. Sprinkle evenly over pears.

Bake until pears are tender and topping is golden, approximately 30–40 minutes. Let cool slightly before serving.

Serve warm or at room temperature. Top with ice cream, if desired.

Variation: Substitute fresh or frozen blueberries, apples, or other fruit for the pears.

Pumpkin Rice Pudding

Fiber-rich pudding perfect for those pumpkin lovers. Pudding can be served for breakfast.

Makes 3-4 servings

- 1 cup pumpkin puree
- 1 cup milk or non-dairy milk of choice
- 1/2 cup cooked brown rice
- 2 tablespoons maple syrup
- 1 teaspoon ground cinnamon
- 1/2 teaspoon vanilla extract
- 1/4 teaspoon ground nutmeg
- 1/8 teaspoon ground cloves
- 1/8 teaspoon ground ginger
- 1 cup blueberries, fresh or frozen

Coat a 3 quart slow cooker with cooking spray.

Assemble all ingredients except blueberries in the slow cooker and mix. Cook on low 3–4 hours.

Add blueberries and cook an additional 30 minutes to blend the flavors.

Serve warm topped with whipped cream, yogurt, or kefir, if desired.

Rhubarb Surprise

Rhubarb has many health benefits. The fiber in rhubarb may lower LDL cholesterol levels without changing HDL levels, so it is good for the heart. This is yummy for desert.

Makes approximately 6 servings

- 2 cups fresh rhubarb stalks or frozen unsweetened rhubarb, sliced into 1-inch pieces
- 2 cups diced pears, apples (peeled or unpeeled), or fresh strawberries
- 1/2 cup dry old-fashioned oats
- 1/3 cup brown sugar
- 3 tablespoons whole wheat flour, white whole wheat flour, or arrowroot

- 2 tablespoons bittersweet or chocolate chips
- 2 tablespoons nuts, chopped (use any nut you like)
- 1 tablespoon oil of choice *or* butter, melted
- 1 teaspoon ground cinnamon
- 1 teaspoon cocoa powder
- 1/2 teaspoon ground ginger
- fresh basil leaves, chopped (optional)

Slow Cooker Method

Coat a 3-quart slow cooker with cooking spray.

Place fruit in slow cooker.

Mix together remaining ingredients and sprinkle over fruit.

Cook on low heat 3–4 hours.

Oven Method

Preheat oven to 350 degrees F.

Place fruit in an 8-inch square pan sprayed with cooking spray. Mix together remaining ingredients and sprinkle over fruit.

Bake 35 minutes, or until fruit is tender and topping is golden.

Serve warm topped with frozen yogurt, whipped cream, ice cream, yogurt kefir, or a topping of your choosing.

Rice Puddings

These fiber-rich puddings can be eaten for breakfast, dessert, or a satisfying snack.

Stove top Rice Pudding

Makes 4 servings

- 2 cups cooked brown rice
- 1 1/2 cups milk or nondairy milk of your choice
- 2–3 tablespoons raisins, dried apricots, blueberries, apples, another fruit of choice, or a combination
- 1 tablespoon maple syrup or appropriate amount of other sweetener
- 1 teaspoon vanilla extract
- 1/2 teaspoon ground cinnamon
- chopped nuts for topping

In a medium saucepan combine all ingredients except nuts. Bring to a slow simmer and cook uncovered, stirring occasionally, about 20 minutes, or until desired consistency.

Serve hot or cold topped with chopped nuts.

Baked Rice Pudding

Makes 6–8 servings

- 2 1/2 cups cooked brown rice
- 1 1/2 cups milk or nondairy milk of your choice
- 1 cup raisins, dried tart cherries, or dried apricots
- 1/4 cup granulated sugar or light brown sugar
- 2 tablespoons oil of choice *or* butter, melted
- 2 eggs
- 1/2 teaspoon vanilla extract
- 1/4 teaspoon ground cinnamon
- 1/4 teaspoon ground nutmeg
- fresh fruit, such as blueberries, raspberries, sliced strawberries, peaches, nectarines, or mango, for topping

Coat a 9 × 13–inch dish with cooking spray.

Combine all ingredients except fresh fruit in a large bowl. Mix well.

Pour into baking dish. Bake until top is golden brown, approximately 30 minutes. Don't overbake.

Top pudding with fresh fruit of your choice. Serve warm or cold.

Sautéed Cinnamon Apples

This recipe makes an excellent fiber-rich snack or light dessert by itself, or you can serve the apples over vanilla ice cream, vanilla yogurt, or plain yogurt. For this recipe, it's better to use a firmer cooking apple, but you can use any apples you like. Use a variety of apples for more flavor. Enjoy!

- apples, approximately 1 apple per person
- butter or oil or choice (optional)
- ground cinnamon
- honey (optional)

Slice apples into thin wedges or slices, preferably not peeling for more nutrition.

Coat a frying pan of sufficient size with cooking spray or use a small amount of butter or oil of choice.

Place apples in pan and sprinkle with ground cinnamon, using as much or as little as you like. I like to use a lot of ground cinnamon.

Slowly sauté apples over low to medium heat, stirring occasionally, until apples achieve desired tenderness and brownness. You may need to add small amounts of water while stirring so the apples won't stick to the pan.

Add a little honey if you like the apples sweeter.

Slow-Cooked Applesauce

My granddaughters, Lily and Ansley, love this recipe! Good apple varieties for this dish include Golden Delicious, Gala, Granny Smith, Braeburn, and Gravenstein, or you can use a combination of varieties. Make sure to wash them well and preferably use organic. This applesauce is great for topping oatmeal or vanilla ice cream and wonderful served with cooked pork.

Makes 4 or more servings

- 2–3 pounds (approximately 8 large) apples, unpeeled and sliced
- scant 1/3 cup water
- 1 cinnamon stick, about 3 inches long
- approximately 1 teaspoon brown sugar (optional; not really needed unless the apples are tart)

Combine all ingredients in a 3-quart to 4-quart slow cooker.

Cook on low 8 hours or on high 3–4 hours. Remove cinnamon stick.

Mash with a potato masher or immersion blender to desired consistency.

Serve warm or cold.

Variation: Add some pumpkin pie spice for a different flavor.

Burgers and Patties

Black Bean Burgers

Tasty alternative to a meat burger

Makes 5 small or 3 large patties

- 1–3 teaspoons oil of choice, divided
- 3/4 cup diced mixed vegetables (zucchini, broccoli, mushrooms, peppers, squash, or corn)
- 1 tablespoon chopped scallions *or* 1/4 cup chopped raw onion
- 1 (15-ounce) can black beans, drained, rinsed, and mashed (may use equivalent amount of beans cooked from dried)
- 1/2 cup old-fashioned oats or bread crumbs
- 1 egg
- 1 teaspoon chili powder
- dash of garlic powder *or* 1 clove of garlic, minced
- black pepper (optional)

Sauté onions and vegetables in a small frying pan in small amount of the oil until softened.

Mix with remaining ingredients in a large bowl. Form into patties. If mixture is not firm, refrigerate for a short time (may be done one day ahead).

Form into patties.

Heat oil in skillet and brown patties on each side until heated through, approximately 2–3 minutes per side.

Serve on toasted buns or with a side dish. Or serve open face over corn or flour tortillas and top with guacamole, sour cream, salsa, cilantro, crumbled goat cheese, Mexican cheese, or other cheese.

Variations:

Use 1 cup of beans and 1 cup of cooked brown rice. Add 2 tablespoons mashed yam, pumpkin, or sweet potato; 2 tablespoons chopped white part of leeks; 1 teaspoon chili powder; 1/2 teaspoon dried basil; and 1/2 teaspoon ground cumin.

Add 1/2 cup minced walnuts for texture, flavor, and added protein.

Add 1 teaspoon or more of soy sauce or Bragg Liquid Aminos for flavor.

Add a handful of minced cilantro or parsley to freshen the flavor.

Top with cheese of choice when second side is cooking.

Garbanzo Bean (Chickpea) Burgers

Healthy, fiber-rich burger.

Makes 4 burgers

- 1 (15-ounce) can garbanzo beans, rinsed and drained, or an equivalent amount of dried garbanzo beans, cooked
- 1/2 cup parsley or cilantro
- 2 tablespoons chopped fresh onion
- 4 large cloves of garlic, chopped (use more if desired)
- 1 teaspoon ground cumin

- 1 egg, slightly beaten
- black pepper to taste
- 6 tablespoons toasted bread crumbs, made from scratch or store bought, divided
- salt (optional)
- cooking spray or oil of choice
- 1/2 cup low fat or nonfat greek-style yogurt
- 1 tablespoon fresh lemon juice

In a food processor or using a food chopper, coarsely chop the garbanzo beans, parsley or cilantro, onion, garlic, and cumin. Mixture should come together.

Transfer mixture to a bowl and add egg and 3 tablespoons bread crumbs. Mix gently.

Shape into 4 large burgers. Put remaining bread crumbs on a plate and gently dip each burger in bread crumbs until coated.

Let burgers sit in refrigerator for a short while before cooking, if you have time.

Meanwhile, mix yogurt and lemon juice to make a sauce and set aside.

Spray a skillet with cooking spray or add some oil. Cook burgers over medium heat 5–10 minutes per side until golden crisp.

Serve with the sauce if desired.

Veggie Patties

These patties are fiber-rich and good with meat, poultry, fish, or eggs. They're also good just by themselves. They're surprisingly yummy for breakfast, as well.

Makes about 8 patties

- 1 1/4 cups shredded unpeeled zucchini, drained in colander and liquid pressed out
- 1 cup shredded carrots, unpeeled if organic
- 1 cup shredded sweet potato, unpeeled if organic
- 1/3–1/2 cup grated parmesan cheese or other cheese of choice
- 2 eggs
- 2 tablespoons old-fashioned oats or bread crumbs
- 1 tablespoon finely chopped red onion *or* 1 teaspoon dried onion flakes
- 1 tablespoon Bragg Liquid Aminos or soy sauce
- 3/4 teaspoon dried oregano
- 3/4 teaspoon garlic powder
- salt and pepper to taste
- cooking spray or a slight amount of oil of choice

Gently mix all ingredients together. Form into patties, using 1/3 cup of mixture per patty.

Coat skillet with cooking spray or add a small amount of oil of your choice. Fry patties 5–10 minutes per side, or to desired crispness.

Serve with sour cream, yogurt, and applesauce, or be creative with your own toppings.

White Bean Burgers

Enjoy them as you would any burger, but reap the fiber benefits.

Makes 4 patties

- 1 (15-ounce) can great northern beans, rinsed and drained (may use equivalent amount of beans cooked from dried)
- 1/2 cup fresh soft bread crumbs made from whole wheat bread or bread of choice
- 1/3 cup chopped parsley
- 1/3 cup grated carrots
- 1/3 cup cooked brown rice
- 1/4 cup chopped red onion
- 1 egg, slightly beaten
- 1 teaspoon Bragg Liquid Aminos or soy sauce
- 1/2 teaspoon dried thyme leaf
- 1/2 teaspoon garlic powder
- salt and pepper to taste
- other seasonings, such as chili powder (optional)
- 1 tablespoon or more oil for frying
- additional bread crumbs to coat patties before frying (optional)
- 1–2 tablespoons grated Parmesan cheese or other cheese (optional)

Mash or puree the beans in a food processor. Transfer to a bowl and add remaining ingredients including grated cheese if using. Mix well.

Form into 4 patties. Refrigerate a little while so patties will hold shape. Before frying, coat patties in additional bread crumbs, if desired.

Fry patties approximately 5–10 minutes per side, or to desired crispness.

Top burgers with sliced cheese, sour cream, or yogurt if desired

Yummy Quinoa Patties

These are a creative way to use quinoa; they are rich in fiber and protein too. Top with some yogurt for a delicious treat.

Makes 10–12 patties

- 2 1/2 cups cooked quinoa, any color
- 1 cup grated carrots
- approximately 1/2 cup finely diced scallions
- 1/2 cup cottage cheese
- 1/2 cup bread crumbs, finely ground
- 1/2 cup old-fashioned oats
- 1/2 cup finely chopped parsley
- 1/2 cup finely chopped kale, tough stems removed
- 3 eggs, slightly beaten
- 1 teaspoon sea salt or salt of choice
- 1 teaspoon chili powder
- 1/2 teaspoon garlic powder
- 1/2 teaspoon pepper
- dash of ground cumin (optional)
- 2 tablespoons oil of choice; use more as needed

Mix all ingredients together. Add a little water if mixture seems dry.

Form mixture into patties, 1/3 cup each.

Add oil to frying pan. Cook patties until brown and crisp, approximately 5–10 minutes per side.

Vegetables

Freekeh Veggie Stir Fry

This stir fry uses freekeh, an ancient, high-fiber grain known for its earthy, smoky flavor and chewy texture. It cooks quickly and might become your new favorite grain. This is a very appealing plant-based, one-pot dish.

Makes 2–4 servings

- 1 tablespoon oil of choice
- 1/3 cup sliced scallions or onion of choice
- 2 garlic cloves, chopped
- 2 cups cubed zucchini or crookneck squash
- 1 cup cherry or grape tomatoes, halved or quartered (depending on size) *or* 1 cup chopped fresh tomato
- 1/3 cup chopped parsley
- 1 1/2 tablespoons balsamic vinegar
- splash of Bragg Liquid Aminos or soy sauce
- 1 cup cooked freekeh, slightly cooled
- additional chopped vegetables (optional)
- sesame seeds or grated cheese for sprinkling on finished dish

Heat oil in medium size skillet over low heat. When oil is ready, add scallions and garlic and cook 2–3 minutes.

Add zucchini or squash and sauté 10–15 minutes until softened and lightly browned. Add additional chopped vegetables if using.

Add tomatoes, parsley, balsamic vinegar, and Bragg Liquid Aminos or soy sauce and cook 5 more minutes.

Stir in the cooked frekeeh and combine well.

Serve hot as a side dish or main dish. Sprinkle sesame seeds or grated cheese on individual servings. Goes well with poultry, seafood, or beef.

Leafy Greens Sauté

Makes a great fiber-rich side dish to poultry, meat, or seafood. It can also serve as a fiber-filled entrée if you add beans.

Makes 2 or more servings

- approximately 1 pound fresh greens (spinach, kale, red or green swiss chard, collard greens, mustard greens, turnip greens, etc.), thoroughly washed and dried *or* equivalent amount of prepackaged greens mix
- 1–2 tablespoons oil of choice
- 4–5 cloves of garlic cloves, minced (more if desired)
- 1 chopped shallot or some chopped onion (optional)
- salt, pepper, and other desired seasonings
- 1 tablespoon lemon juice (optional)
- chopped nuts, sesame seeds, or pine nuts for topping
- grated cheese of choice for topping

Remove tough stems from greens, if necessary, and tear or cut into appropriate size pieces.

Heat the oil in a wok, skillet, or saucepan over medium heat. When warm enough, add garlic and shallots or onions (if using). Sauté until translucent.

Add greens and toss well. Cover and cook until greens are wilted and tender, approximately 5 minutes.

Uncover and cook a few minutes longer to reduce excess liquid. Add seasonings and lemon juice (if using). Stir gently.

Sprinkle with the desired toppings and serve.

Quick Leafy Greens Stir Fry

This is a quick and easy fiber-rich meal for a lunch or dinner.

Makes 3–4 servings, approximately 1 cup each

- small amount of cooking oil of choice
- a few cloves of garlic, sliced
- 4 cups chopped kale, collard greens, swiss chard, escarole, or greens of choice with tough stems removed, washed (use washed and precut greens to save time)
- 2 cups cooked brown rice, barley, wheat berries, or whole grain of choice
- 1 tablespoon or more Bragg Liquid Aminos, soy sauce, or sauce of choice

Sauté sliced garlic in oil in a medium skillet over low heat until golden brown.

Add leafy greens and cook until bright green and wilted.

Stir in the cooked whole grain. Simmer until desired texture or tenderness.

Add Bragg Liquid Aminos, soy sauce, or other sauce just before serving.

Serve topped with sesame seeds, pumpkin seeds, grated cheese, or whatever strikes your imagination.

Variation: Add some other spices and diced poultry, meat, or seafood for additional protein.

Roasted Vegetables

No fiber-rich cookbook would be complete without a recipe for roasted vegetables. Use any combination of vegetables you like. Roasting is a great way to cook some vegetables. It brings out their sweetness and natural flavor. Create away; experiment to see which vegetables complement each other.

Makes 5–6 servings

- 5–6 cups vegetables
- 2 tablespoons oil of choice
- 1 tablespoon balsamic vinegar, Bragg Liquid Aminos, or soy sauce
- spices of choice, such as salt, pepper, garlic powder, italian seasoning, dried thyme leaf, dried basil, dried oregano, or ground cinnamon
- garlic, minced (optional)
- lemon zest (optional)

Vegetable suggestions: broccoli or cauliflower, broken into florets; red potatoes, sweet potatoes, or fingerling potatoes, cut into chunks; butternut squash or pumpkin, cut into 1-inch cubes; brussels sprouts with bottoms cut off, sliced in halves or quarters; carrots, parsnips, turnips, or rutabagas, peeled and sliced into 1-inch pieces; leeks, cut into chunks; eggplant, cut into chunks; shallots or red onion sliced; peeled beets, cut into cubes; asparagus pieces; sweet peppers; green beans.

Preheat oven to 400 degrees F.

Start with a large roasting pan. Coat with cooking spray or line with parchment paper or foil; spray the liner with cooking spray for easier clean up.

Place vegetables in a single layer in pan. Drizzle vegetable mixture with oil and balsamic vinegar, Bragg Liquid Aminos, or soy sauce. Sprinkle with spices. Add minced garlic or lemon zest on top if desired. Toss well.

Roast approximately 40–60 minutes or more until vegetables are tender and golden on edges. Turn occasionally while roasting for even browning. When roasting a variety of vegetables, you may have to add the more delicate ones, which take less time to cook, to the pan 10–15 minutes into the cooking process so all vegetables are done at the same time.

After roasting, add more seasonings or a splash of lemon juice if desired. Garnish with finely chopped parsley, grated cheese, sesame seeds, or chopped nuts to enhance your creation.

Warm One-pot Dishes

Chickpea Stew

This recipe can be made on the stove or assembled and cooked in a slow cooker.

Makes 4 servings

- 2 tablespoons oil of choice
- 1 cup diced red or yellow onion
- 2 tablespoons finely chopped garlic
- 1 teaspoon ground cumin
- 2 (15-ounce) cans chickpeas, rinsed and drained *or* 3 cups chickpeas cooked from dried
- 1 (14.5-ounce) can diced tomatoes, undrained

- 1 1/4 cups chicken broth or stock (use only 1/2 cup if using the slow cooker)
- 1 tablespoon lemon juice
- 1 teaspoon honey
- 1 teaspoon dried thyme leaf
- 1/2 teaspoon dried oregano
- salt, pepper, and other seasonings as desired
- 1/2 cup chopped parsley or kale

Heat oil over low heat in a medium size pot. Add onion and cook until almost translucent, approximately 8–10 minutes. Add garlic and cook another 5 minutes.

Stir in cumin and cook 2 more minutes.

Transfer to slow cooker, if using that method, along with remaining ingredients except parsley or kale and cook on low 5–6 hours.

If cooking on stovetop, add remaining ingredients except parsley or kale to pot and bring to a boil. Skim off any foam that may form. Reduce heat and simmer until sauce thickens somewhat, approximately 20 minutes.

Stir in the parsley or kale just before serving. Delicious served over brown rice, couscous or grain of choice.

Variation: add some zucchini cut into 1/2-inch pieces when adding chickpeas and tomatoes.

Eggplant One-pot Stew

A quick and easy fiber-rich meal. Delicious served over rice or barley.

Makes 4 servings

- 3 cups eggplant cut into 1/2-inch cubes, peeled or unpeeled
- 1 cup sliced carrots
- 1 cup sliced celery
- 1 cup chopped red onion
- 4 cloves of garlic, minced
- 2 cups coarsely chopped fresh tomatoes
- 2 cups cubed sweet potatoes, peeled or unpeeled
- 1 1/2 cups canned red kidney beans, rinsed and drained *or* beans cooked from dried
- 1 (15-ounce) can tomato sauce
- 3 cups broth or stock of choice (I used chicken)
- 1 bay leaf
- 1 teaspoon ground cinnamon
- 1/2 teaspoon dried oregano
- 1/2 teaspoon dried basil
- salt and pepper to taste
- additional spices if desired
- 1/2 cup chopped parsley for topping
- grated cheese of choice, such as feta, or sesame seeds for topping

Spray slow cooker with cooking spray to prevent sticking. Assemble all ingredients except toppings in slow cooker. Cook on low 9–10 hours or on high 5–6 hours.

The toppings add flavor and appeal.

Eggplant Stew

Italian flair with a healthy dose of fiber.

Makes 4 servings

- 3 cups unpeeled eggplant diced into 3/4-inch cubes, preferably organic
- salt
- 1 tablespoon of oil of choice
- 2/3 cup chopped white onion
- 3 large cloves garlic, minced or pressed
- 1/2 cup chopped fresh tomato chopped *or* canned diced tomatoes, drained
- 1 bay leaf
- 1 teaspoon dried oregano
- 1/2 teaspoon dried thyme leaf
- 1/4 teaspoon curry powder (optional)
- a few dashes of Bragg Liquid Aminos or soy sauce (optional)
- chopped parsley (optional)
- sesame seeds (optional)

Place cubed eggplant in a bowl and sprinkle with salt. Cover and refrigerate at least an hour. Rinse and lightly squeeze eggplant, and then dry.

Preheat oven to 400 degrees F. Coat a 2-3 quart casserole dish with cooking spray.

Heat oil in a skillet. Sauté garlic and onion over low heat briefly to soften.

Combine eggplant with garlic and onion. Add tomatoes and seasonings, as well as Bragg Liquid Aminos or soy sauce if using. Mix well.

Pour mixture into casserole dish and bake 30–40 minutes, or until eggplant is soft and flavors are blended.

Remove bay leaf and serve.

Savory Red Lentils and Brown Rice Stew

A hearty, fiber-rich, and savory one-pot meal.

Makes 4 hearty servings

- 1/2 tablespoon oil of choice
- 1 small onion, chopped (approximately 1/2 cup)
- 3 cloves garlic, minced *or* 3/8 teaspoon garlic powder
- 1 teaspoon ground cumin
- 1 teaspoon ground cinnamon
- 1/4 teaspoon pepper
- 1/2 teaspoon ground ginger
- 1/4 teaspoon salt (optional)
- 4 cups hot water or chicken broth or stock
- 1 cup uncooked brown rice, rinsed
- 1 cup split red lentils, rinsed and sorted for stones
- 3 medium carrots, chopped (approximately 1 1/2 cups)
- 1 1/2 cups cherry tomatoes, halved *or* chopped fresh tomatoes
- 1 cup sliced zucchini
- 1/3 cup snipped or chopped fresh parsley or cilantro
- 1 cup sweet potatoes cut into 1 inch cubes, peeled if not organic (optional)
- 1 (9-ounce) bag fresh spinach *or* 1 (10-ounce) package frozen leaf spinach, thawed and squeezed dry
- 2 tablespoons lemon juice (optional)
- 4 ounces mozzarella cheese or cheese of choice, shredded

In a large saucepan heat oil slightly. Add onion, garlic cloves or powder, cinnamon, cumin, ginger, and pepper, as well as salt, if using. Cook approximately 10 minutes until lightly browned.

Add liquid, rice, lentils, carrots, tomatoes, and zucchini, as well as sweet potatoes and lemon juice, if using. Bring to a boil.

Reduce heat and simmer 45 minutes, or until lentils, rice, and potatoes are tender. Stir in parsley or cilantro and spinach and continue cooking until wilted.

Add cheese and serve.

Spelt Stew to Warm You

This unusual, simple, and hearty stew is a great way to enjoy chewy, nutty, fiber-rich spelt berries; try it for an unusual one-pot, fiber-rich dish.

Makes 4–6 servings

- 1 cup spelt berries
- 1 tablespoon oil of choice
- 1 cup chopped onion
- 1/2 cup diced celery
- 1 cup diced carrots
- 4 garlic cloves, minced
- 3–4 cups peeled, diced winter squash (such as butternut, acorn, or kabocha)
- 4 cups chicken broth or stock

- 3 cups coarsely chopped fresh kale or spinach, washed (stems removed from kale)
- 2 cups beans, cooked from dried *or* canned beans, rinsed and drained (works well with black or white beans, but just use your favorite)
- 1 (14.5-ounce) can diced tomatoes, undrained
- 1 bay leaf
- 1 teaspoon dried thyme leaf
- 1/2 teaspoon salt (optional)
- 1/2 teaspoon black pepper (optional)
- additional seasonings as desired
- grated cheese of choice and minced parsley for garnish

Soak spelt berries in water several hours or overnight. Drain and set aside.

Sauté onion, celery, carrots, and garlic cloves in oil in a large pot over low heat until tender.

Add drained spelt and diced squash and sauté 10 minutes more.

Add chicken broth or stock. Add bay leaf and seasonings. Bring to a boil. Reduce heat and simmer covered until spelt and squash are tender, approximately 40 minutes.

Add kale or spinach. Simmer until the kale or spinach is wilted.

Add beans and tomatoes. Simmer covered awhile longer for flavors to blend. Adjust seasonings if necessary. Remove bay leaf.

Serve topped with cheese and sprinkled with chopped parsley.

White Bean Stew

Serve with a salad and crusty bread for a hearty, fiber-rich meal.

Makes 8 servings

- 1 tablespoon oil of choice
- 1 1/2–2 cups chopped onions
- 1 cup sliced carrots
- 1/2 cup sliced celery
- 3 cloves of garlic, chopped
- 1 tablespoon italian seasoning
- 1 teaspoon chili powder
- 4 cups chicken broth or stock
- 3 cups white beans of choice, cooked from dried *or* 2 (15-ounce) cans beans, rinsed and drained (works well with small white beans)
- 1 cup chopped fresh tomatoes *or* canned diced tomatoes, drained
- 2 cups coarsely chopped parsley or kale
- slight amount of lemon juice (optional)
- grated cheese or sesame seeds for topping

Place oil in medium size pot and heat slightly over low heat. Add onions, carrots, celery, garlic, Italian seasoning, and chili powder. Sauté stirring frequently until slightly cooked, approximately 15 minutes. Be careful not to let burn.

Add broth or stock, beans and tomatoes. Bring to a boil. Reduce heat and simmer covered 30–45 minutes.

Add parsley or kale and simmer covered an additional 10 minutes, or until greens are tender. Add lemon juice, if using.

Serve warm topped with cheese or sesame seeds.

Variation: Add some sliced cooked sausage or cut up chicken.

Quick Tomato Garbanzo Bean Sauté

This is a quick, satisfying, fiber-rich meal.

Makes 1–2 servings

- 1 teaspoon oil of choice
- 1 cup diced fresh tomato
- 1/2 cup diced onion
- 1/4 teaspoon dried thyme leaf
- 1/4 teaspoon dried basil
- 1/4 teaspoon dried oregano
- Red pepper flakes if more heat is desired
- Salt, pepper to taste
- 1 cup garbanzo beans from canned, rinsed and drained or cooked from dried

Sauté onions, tomato, and herbs in oil in a small pot over low heat until tender.

Stir in garbanzo beans. Cover and simmer over low heat until warmed.

Serve over rice or quinoa. Sprinkle cheese, sesame seeds, pumpkins seeds, pine nuts, or chopped nuts on top if desired

Quick and Easy Vegetarian Bean Chili

Great for a quick meal on a chilly day.

Makes 2 large servings

- small amount of oil of choice (optional)
- 1 cup chopped onion
- 2 garlic cloves, chopped
- 1 (14.5-ounce) can diced tomatoes, undrained
- 1 cup water
- 1 cup black beans, red beans, or white beans, cooked from dried *or* canned beans, rinsed and drained
- 2/3 cup black-eyed peas, cooked from dried *or* canned black-eyed peas, rinsed and drained
- 1/3 cup tomato paste
- 1 tablespoon chili powder
- 1/4 teaspoon ground cumin
- additional seasonings as desired
- shredded cheese or sesame seeds (optional)

Sauté onion and garlic in a little oil or water in a medium saucepan over low heat until softened. (If you are in a real hurry, you can skip this step and simply boil the raw onion and garlic with the other ingredients.)

Add water, tomatoes, beans, black-eyed peas, tomato paste, chili powder, and cumin. Bring to a boil.

Reduce heat and simmer covered 20–30 minutes.

Sprinkle each serving with cheese or sesame seeds if desired.

Hearty Sweet Potato Black Bean Chili

This is a yummy tummy warmer.

Makes approximately 6 servings

- 1 tablespoon olive oil or oil of choice
- 1 cup chopped onion
- 2 teaspoons chili powder
- 1 teaspoon ground cumin
- 1/4 teaspoon garlic powder
- 2 large sweet potatoes (approximately 1 pound) scrubbed and cut into 1/2-inch cubes equaling approximately 3–4 cups
- 2 (14.5-ounce) cans diced tomatoes, undrained
- 2 (15-ounce) cans black beans, drained and rinsed *or* 3 cups black beans cooked from dried

Stove Top Method

Cook onions in oil in a large pot over medium heat until lightly browned.

Stir in chili powder, cumin, and garlic powder and cook approximately 5 minutes.

Add sweet potatoes and tomatoes. Bring to a slight boil

Reduce heat and simmer until sweet potatoes are partially cooked, approximately 10 minutes.

Add black beans. Simmer covered 30–60 minutes on low heat until sweet potatoes are tender and flavors are blended.

Slow Cooker Method

Assemble all ingredients in a slow cooker and cook on low for 6-8 hours.

Variation: You can use canned diced tomatoes with green chilies instead of plain tomatoes or add some canned diced green chilies to the chili mixture for a spicier taste.

Lentil Chili

Freeze some for a quick, nutritious, fiber-rich meal.

Makes 4 servings

- 1/4 cup chopped onion
- 2 cloves garlic, minced
- 2 teaspoons ground cumin
- 1 tablespoon chili powder
- 1/4 teaspoon dried oregano
- 2 cups water or vegetable broth or stock
- 3/4 cup green, brown, black, or red lentils, rinsed and drained
- 1/2 cup chopped fresh tomatoes *or* canned diced tomatoes, drained
- 1 cup peeled and diced butternut squash (optional)
- 1/2 cup diced green pepper (optional)
- 2 teaspoons lime juice (optional)
- Suggested toppings: cheddar cheese, pumpkin seeds, thinly sliced scallions or chopped cilantro (optional)

Slow Cooker Method

Coat a 3-quart to 4-quart slow cooker with cooking spray to prevent sticking.

Assemble all ingredients except lime juice and toppings in slow cooker and cook covered on low 8–10 hours or on high 5–6 hours.

Stir in lime juice if using. Ladle into bowls, and sprinkle your choice of toppings on each serving.

Stove Top Method

Heat a small of amount of oil of choice in a large saucepan over medium heat. Add garlic and onions and cook, stirring, until softened.

Stir in seasonings and cook additional 5 minutes.

Add broth or stock, lentils, and tomatoes. Bring to a boil. Reduce the heat and simmer uncovered 30 minutes.

Stir in squash and green pepper (if using). Continue simmering until lentils, squash, and green pepper are tender. Stir in lime juice if using.

Ladle into bowls and top with desired toppings.

Lentil-Bulgur Slow Cooker Combo

Makes 4 servings

- 2 cups water, chicken broth, or vegetable broth or stock
- 1/2 cup fresh or frozen corn
- 1/2 cup bulgur wheat
- 1/4 cup lentils (preferably red)
- 1/2 teaspoon ground cumin
- 1/2 teaspoon garlic powder
- 3/4 cup chopped fresh tomatoes
- 1/2 cup chopped parsley or cilantro
- grated cheese for topping
- Assemble liquid, corn, bulgur wheat, lentils, and spices in a 3-quart slow cooker. Cook 3–4 hours on low.
- Add tomatoes and parsley or cilantro. Cook an additional 15–30 minutes on low.
- Serve warm from the slow cooker or cold. Sprinkle individual servings with some cheese if desired (good with feta).

Lentil Stew

Leftovers can be eaten wrapped in tortillas or pita bread.

Makes 4 servings

- 1 tablespoon oil of choice *or* small amount of cooking spray
- 1 (14.5-ounce) can diced tomatoes, undrained
- 1 cup dried green, brown, or black lentils, rinsed and drained
- 1 cup chopped zucchini
- 1 cup chopped cauliflower
- 1 cup chopped carrots
- 1/2 cup chopped celery
- 1/2 cup chopped scallions
- 3–5 cloves garlic, chopped
- 2 tablespoons balsamic vinegar
- 1/2 teaspoon ground cumin
- 1/2 teaspoon paprika
- salt, pepper, and other seasonings to taste
- grated cheese or sesame seeds for topping

Heat oil or cooking spray in a large saucepan over medium heat. Add remaining ingredients except toppings and stir a few minutes. Bring to a boil.

Reduce heat to a simmer. Cover and cook 30–45 minutes, or until ingredients are tender.

Serve over brown rice, barley, or farro. Sprinkle with cheese or sesame seeds, if desired.

Zesty Lentils

Easy and quick way to cook a fiber-rich dish in one pot using the rice cooker or stove.

Makes 4 main-dish servings or 8 side-dish servings

- 1 1/2 cups water, vegetable broth or stock
- 1 (8-ounce) can tomato sauce
- 1/2 cup lentils, rinsed and drained (green work best)
- 1/2 cup diced carrot
- 1/2 cup diced celery
- 1/2 cup diced fresh tomato
- 1 tablespoon dried onion flakes *or* equivalent amount chopped onions
- 1 tablespoon dried parsley flakes *or* equivalent amount chopped fresh parsley
- 1/2 teaspoon garlic powder
- 1/2 teaspoon ground cumin
- 1/4 teaspoon curry powder
- grated cheese or sesame seeds for topping

Lightly coat a medium size pot or rice cooker with cooking spray.

Add all ingredients except topping.

If using rice cooker, just cook until done. If cooking in pot on stove top, bring to a boil, stir, and lower heat, simmering about 30–40 minutes until tender.

Sprinkle individual servings with grated cheese, sesame seeds, or both, if desired.

Lentil Barley Stew

This is an easy and quick fiber-rich stew to make. For a complete meal, serve this hearty stew with a green salad. It is wonderful for leftovers and freezes well. It may thicken after a day in the refrigerator

Makes 4–6 servings

- 2 teaspoons oil of choice *or* small amount of cooking spray
- 1/2 cup chopped onion
- 1/2 cup chopped celery
- 1/2 cup chopped carrot
- 4–5 cloves of garlic minced
- 3 cups water *or* 3 cups vegetable or chicken broth or stock (much richer with the broth or stock)
- 1 (14.5-ounce) can diced tomatoes, undrained
- 1/2 cup dry lentils, rinsed (preferably green or brown)
- 1/3 cup dry hulled or pearl barley, rinsed
- 1 tablespoon minced fresh parsley *or* 1 teaspoon dried parsley
- 1 teaspoon balsamic vinegar
- 3/4 teaspoon dried oregano
- 3/4 teaspoon ground cumin
- 1/8 teaspoon crushed red pepper (optional)
- salt to taste
- 2 bay leaves
- additional seasonings if desired

Coat a medium pot with cooking spray or add oil. Add onion, celery, carrot, and garlic and cook over medium heat until softened, stirring.

Add remaining ingredients and bring to a slow boil. Cover and simmer about 1 hour, or until lentils and barley are soft. Add more liquid if desired for soupier consistency.

Add additional seasonings as desired.

Linda's Saucy Red Lentils and Corn

This is a quick, easy, one-pot vegetarian meal. Serve it with a salad and a vegetable on the side for a delicious and nutritious meal.

Makes 4 servings, 1 cup lentil mixture and 1/2 cup grain each

- 1 tablespoon grapeseed oil or oil of choice
- 1 medium yellow onion, chopped (approximately 1/2–1 cup)
- 4 garlic cloves, chopped
- 1 1/2 cups vegetable broth or stock (or use chicken broth or stock for a richer flavor)

- 1/2 cup dried red lentils, rinsed
- 1 tablespoon chili powder
- 1 1/2 teaspoons ground cumin
- 1 cup frozen corn, preferably organic or use cooked fresh corn
- 1 cup tomato sauce
- 1/3 cup tomato paste
- 1 teaspoon dried oregano
- 1 teaspoon red wine vinegar
- 2 cups hot cooked brown rice, wild rice, barely, or farro
- 3/4 cup shredded cheddar cheese or cheese of choice

Coat a medium size saucepan with cooking spray. Add oil and sauté onion and garlic over low heat until tender, approximately 5–10 minutes.

Add the broth or stock, red lentils, chili powder, and cumin. Slowly bring to a boil and then reduce heat. Cover and simmer 30 minutes, or until lentils are almost tender.

Stir in corn, tomato sauce, tomato paste, oregano, and vinegar. Slowly return to boil and then reduce heat again. Cover and simmer 10 minutes more, or until the lentils are tender.

Serve over rice, barley, or farro. Sprinkle the cheese on top.

Variation: Substitute salsa for tomato sauce for more zip.

Slow Cooker Ratatouille with Lentils

Delicious served over brown rice, barely, or farro, this is a very comforting meal on a cold day.

Makes approximately 3–4 servings

- 2 cups cubed eggplant, peeled if not organic (approximately 6 ounces or 1/2 a small eggplant)
- 1 (14.5-ounce) can diced tomatoes, undrained
- 1 1/2 cups peeled and cubed butternut squash
- 1 medium zucchini or yellow summer squash, halved lengthwise and cut into 1/2-inch slices (approximately 1 1/2 cups)
- 1 large onion, coarsely chopped (approximately 1 cup)
- 1/2 cup dry green or brown lentils, rinsed and drained
- 1/4 cup water
- 1/2 teaspoon garlic powder or use several minced garlic cloves
- 1/2 teaspoon dried oregano
- 1/2 teaspoon dried basil
- 1/2 teaspoon chili powder or adjust to taste
- 1/4 teaspoon ground cumin
- dash of black pepper
- grated cheese or sesame seeds for garnish

Combine all ingredients except garnish in a 3-quart or 4-quart slow cooker.

Cover and cook on low 8–9 hours or on high 4-5 hours. Don't overcook, or it will be mushy.

Serve warm. Garnish individual servings with some grated cheese or sesame seeds.

Zucchini, Black Bean, and Rice Quick Skillet

This is a delicious, fiber-rich one-pot dish. Great for potluck dinners or buffets.

Makes 4–6 main dish servings, approximately 1 1/4 cups each

- 1 tablespoon oil of choice
- 1 1/2 cups cubed zucchini
- 1/2 cup chopped red onion
- 3 cloves garlic chopped
- 1 (15-ounce) can black beans, drained and rinsed *or* approximately 2 cups black beans, cooked from dried

- 1 (14.5-ounce) can diced tomatoes, drained (may use fire roasted with garlic if you want it spicier)
- 2 cups cooked brown rice
- 1 cup fresh or frozen corn
- some diced green pepper (optional)
- 1/2 teaspoon chili powder
- 1/4 teaspoon ground cumin
- 1/2 cup shredded cheese (Cheddar/Monterey Jack blend works well but use any cheese of choice)

Heat oil in a large skillet over medium heat. Add zucchini, onion, and garlic. Cook, stirring, until limp and slightly browned.

Add beans, tomatoes, rice, corn, green pepper (if using), and spices. Stir well. Cover and cook until heated through.

Sprinkle with cheese. Serve after cheese melts.

Quinoa with Peas and Corn

A fiber-rich and tasty one-pot dish. Easily doubled.

Makes 2 servings

- 1/2 cup quinoa, rinsed well
- 1 cup water or vegetable broth
- 1 teaspoon olive oil or oil of choice (optional)
- 4 green onions, sliced
- 3 cloves garlic, chopped
- 1/2–1 teaspoon curry powder, or to taste
- 1/3–1/2 cup chopped fresh tomato
- 1/3 cup fresh or frozen peas
- 1/3 cup fresh or frozen corn
- 1/3 cup diced bell pepper (optional)
- 1/4 cup chopped parsley (may use more)
- 1 teaspoon Bragg Liquid Aminos or soy sauce to taste
- 1 tablespoon lemon juice (optional)

Put quinoa and water or vegetable broth into a medium size pot. Bring to a boil. Reduce heat and simmer about 10 minutes. Turn off heat and let rest 5 minutes, or until all liquid is absorbed. (May also cook quinoa in a rice cooker according to directions.)

While quinoa is cooking, coat a medium size pan in cooking spray or add oil. Sauté green onions, garlic, and curry until lightly browned.

Add tomatoes, peas, corn, bell pepper (if using), and parsley. Cook another 5–10 minutes.

Stir in cooked quinoa and Bragg Liquid Aminos. Stir in lemon juice for more zing, if desired.

Best served warm, but may be eaten cold. Serve as a main dish or side dish.

Salads and Tabboulehs from Legumes, Grains and Pasta

Barley Salad

Barley is rich in phytochemicals, fiber, and minerals. This salad makes a fabulous and nutritious side dish or main course.

Makes 4 servings

- 2 cups cooked barley, pearled or any type you choose
- 1 cup chopped unpeeled tomato
- 1 cup peeled and chopped cucumber
- 2 tablespoons chopped cilantro, parsley, or basil
- 2 tablespoons olive oil or oil of choice
- 2 tablespoons red wine vinegar, apple cider vinegar, rice wine vinegar, or lemon juice
- 1 teaspoon chopped fresh dill or 1/4 teaspoon dried dill
- 1/2 teaspoon garlic powder
- other seasonings as desired to taste
- Optional additions: 2 tablespoons dried cranberries or dried cherries for color and sweetness; approximately 1/2 cup grated carrot; chopped scallions; walnuts or other nuts, chopped; celery, diced or sliced; a few mushrooms, chopped; cooked chicken, turkey, or seafood, diced.

Mix all ingredients together in a mixing bowl. Let rest at least 30 minutes before serving to blend.

Black Bean Salad with a Twist

This salad is good for lunch and surprisingly good for breakfast.

Makes 4 servings

- 1 1/2 cups black beans, cooked from dried *or* 1 (15-ounce) can black beans, drained and rinsed
- 1 cup cooked brown rice, preferably basmati
- 1 cup shredded carrots
- 1 cup chopped fresh tomato
- 2 tablespoons olive oil or oil of choice
- 2 tablespoons red wine vinegar
- 1 scallion, sliced thin (approximately 1 tablespoon)
- black pepper to taste
- other seasonings as desired
- 1 cup cottage cheese, regular, low fat or fat free

Stir together all ingredients except cottage cheese. Let sit 10 minutes for flavors to blend. Gently add the cottage cheese.

Keeps well in an airtight container in refrigerator for a few days.

Black Bean, Rice, and Feta Cheese Salad

The beans and rice together create a complete protein and provide fiber. This salad is a tasty, nutritious meal.

Makes 5 servings

- 2 cups black beans, cooked from dried *or* 1 (15-ounce) can black beans, rinsed and drained
- 1 1/2 cups cooked brown rice, preferably basmati
- 1 1/2 cups chopped fresh tomato
- 1/2 cup feta cheese (regular, reduced fat, or fat free)
- 1/3 cup chopped celery
- 1/3 cup peeled and chopped cucumber
- 1/3 cup chopped scallions
- 1/4 cup red wine vinegar
- 1/4 cup olive oil or oil of choice
- 2 tablespoons chopped fresh cilantro or parsley
- 1/4 teaspoon garlic powder
- black pepper to taste

Mix all ingredients together. Refrigerate awhile to allow flavors to blend. Adjust seasonings to taste if necessary.

Black Bean Quinoa Salad Southwestern Style

This salad is packed with fiber and protein.

Makes 4 servings

- 1 cup quinoa, rinsed
- 1 (15-ounce) can, black beans, rinsed and drained *or* 1 1/2 cups black beans, cooked from dried
- 1 cup peeled and diced cucumber
- 1/2 cup chopped parsley or cilantro
- 1/2 cup chopped tomatoes (optional)
- 1/3 cup diced celery
- 2 tablespoons chopped scallions
- 3 tablespoons red wine vinegar
- 2 tablespoons extra virgin olive oil or oil of choice
- 1 tablespoon yellow mustard
- 2 teaspoons honey or maple syrup
- 1 teaspoon ground cumin
- 1/2 teaspoon garlic powder
- salt and pepper to taste

Cook quinoa in water on stove top or in rice cooker until tender and fluffy. Cool the quinoa slightly.

Mix quinoa, beans, cucumber, parsley or cilantro, tomatoes (if using), and celery in a large bowl.

In a separate bowl, mix together vinegar, oil, mustard, honey or maple syrup, cumin, garlic powder, salt, and pepper. Pour over other ingredients and mix well. You may not need all the dressing, so add as much or as little as you want.

Variations:

Add some diced bell pepper (red, green, yellow or orange), 1/2–1 cup corn, 1/2 cup peeled jicama, or a combination.

Substitute lime juice for the vinegar.

Add chopped jalapeno pepper to spice it up.

Black-Eyed Peas Salad

Black-eyed peas are actually a white bean with a small black dot resembling an eye. They're often used in Southern cooking. Many cultures believe that eating black-eyed peas on New Year's Day will bring prosperity and luck in the new year. They are often overlooked as a tasty, fiber-rich food.

Makes approximately 5 servings, 1/2 cup each

- 1 cup cooked black-eyed peas *or* canned black-eyed peas, drained and rinsed
- 3/4 cooked wild rice, brown rice of your choice, barley, or farro
- 1/2 cup diced fresh tomato
- 1/3 cup chopped red onion
- 1/3 cup chopped celery
- 2 tablespoons diced dried apricots
- 2 tablespoons chopped fresh parsley, cilantro, or basil
- 2 tablespoons lemon juice
- 1 tablespoon grape seed oil or oil of choice
- 1/4 teaspoon garlic powder *or* 1 clove fresh garlic, crushed
- 1/8 teaspoon salt

Combine black-eyed peas, grain of choice, tomato, red onion, celery, apricots, and parsley, cilantro, or basil in a bowl.

In a separate bowl, mix together lemon juice, oil, garlic, and salt. Pour over other ingredients and toss gently.

Chill 1–2 hours if possible before serving.

Variation: Leave out rice, barley, or farro and use more black-eyed peas instead.

Brown Rice Lentil Salad

This is a super-satisfying lunch full of fiber and complete protein.

Makes 4 servings

- 1/2 cup uncooked brown rice, rinsed and drained
- 1/2 cup green lentils, rinsed and drained
- 1 tablespoon oil of choice
- 1/2 cup chopped red or yellow onions *or* chopped scallions
- 2 cloves of garlic chopped
- 1 cup chopped fresh tomatoes
- 1 tablespoon vinegar, red wine, rice wine or apple cider
- 1 tablespoon Bragg Liquid Aminos or soy sauce
- 1 teaspoon ground ginger
- salt and pepper to taste
- dash of dry mustard, dried thyme leaf, or both (optional)
- 2 tablespoons chopped parsley, cilantro, or fresh basil.

In a medium size pot, cook rice and lentils together in 2 cups water, chicken broth, or chicken stock 40–50 minutes until the liquid is absorbed and rice and lentils are tender. (May alternatively cook rice and lentils in a rice cooker until done or in a covered casserole at 350 degrees F for 45 minutes.)

Transfer rice and lentils to a large bowl and fluff. Set aside.

In a pan, sauté onions and garlic in oil. Add to rice and lentil mixture and mix together.

Add tomatoes, vinegar, Bragg Liquid Aminos or soy sauce, ground ginger, salt, pepper, and other spices (if using). Mix well.

Add parsley, cilantro, or fresh basil and gently stir.

Serve hot or cold.

Buckwheat Salad

Buckwheat is a great source of insoluble fiber, and it's gluten free.

Makes 4-6 servings

- 1 cup whole buckwheat groats
- 1/2 cup scallions chopped
- 1/2 cup peeled and chopped cucumber
- 1/3 cup raisins, dried cranberries, or dried cherries
- 1/3 cup fresh parsley or basil, chopped
- 1/4 cup oil of choice
- 1/4 cup lemon juice
- 1 teaspoon curry powder
- 1/2 teaspoon ground turmeric (optional)
- 1/4 teaspoon ground ginger

Cook buckwheat groats in 2 cups water 10–12 minutes. Let stand 5 minutes after cooking. Drain off remaining liquid and then chill. (Should yield approximately 3 1/2 cups)

Combine all ingredients in a bowl by stirring gently. Chill several hours to allow flavors to blend.

Variation: Add seafood, such as tuna, or poultry, such as chicken or turkey, for more protein if desired. Be creative and experiment with each.

Chopped Vegetable Bean Salad

Light, refreshing, and very healthy!

Makes 4 servings

- 1 cup beans, cooked from dried *or* canned beans, rinsed and drained (I use garbanzo)
- 1/2 cup sliced celery
- 1/2 cup chopped fresh tomatoes
- 1/2 cup peeled and chopped cucumber
- 1/2 cup chopped bell pepper
- 1/3–1/2 cup cubed avocado (optional)
- 3 tablespoons chopped parsley or cilantro
- 2 tablespoons shredded carrots (optional)
- 1 tablespoon olive oil or oil of choice
- 1 tablespoon chopped red onion or scallions
- 1 tablespoon lemon juice or red wine vinegar
- 1/2 teaspoon sugar, honey or sweetener of choice
- 1/2 teaspoon garlic powder
- salt (optional)
- additional seasonings to taste

Place all ingredients in a large bowl and gently mix well. Cover and chill 4–24 hours before serving.

Cooling Farro Salad

Farro is a hearty ancient grain with a nutty flavor. It is high in fiber, protein, and iron and is very easy to digest. Makes a great lunch.

Makes 4 or more servings

- 2 1/2 cups cooked farro (about 1 cup uncooked)
- 1 1/2 cups great northern beans, garbanzo beans, or beans of choice, cooked from dried *or* canned beans, rinsed and drained
- 1 cup cherry tomatoes, halved *or* diced fresh tomato
- 1 cup frozen peas, thawed
- 1/2 cup coarsely chopped parsley or other fresh hearty greens, like kale, chard, spinach, or mustard greens
- 1/4 cup chopped scallions
- 3 tablespoons lemon juice
- 2 tablespoons olive oil or oil of choice
- 2 teaspoons Bragg Liquid Aminos or soy sauce
- 1 teaspoon lemon zest
- 1 teaspoon garlic powder
- 1/4 teaspoon ground ginger
- other seasonings to taste
- feta or goat cheese for topping

Combine all ingredients except cheese in a large bowl and gently mix well.

Best served cold. Crumble feta or goat cheese over individual servings.

Freekeh Salad (Cold)

Freekeh is an often overlooked fiber-rich ancient grain. Try it. You will like it.

Makes 3–4 servings

- 1 cup uncooked freekeh, cooked according to package directions
- 1 cup chopped tomatoes *or* quartered cherry tomatoes
- 1/2 cup chopped celery
- 1/2 cup peeled and chopped cucumber
- 1/4 cup chopped parsley, fresh basil, or kale
- 2 tablespoons sliced green onions
- 1 1/2 tablespoons lemon juice
- 1 tablespoon olive oil or oil of choice
- 1 teaspoon balsamic vinegar, apple cider vinegar, or red wine vinegar
- seasonings of choice, such as salt, pepper, and garlic powder
- feta or goat cheese for topping (optional)

Allow freekeh to sit at least 5 minutes after cooking, then fluff with fork.

Mix together all ingredients.

Chill before serving. Top each serving with feta or goat cheese, if desired.

Variation: For a different taste, add some black beans, cooked butternut squash, dried cherries, dried cranberries, or diced apple (peeled or unpeeled).

High Fiber Cold Pasta Salad

Create a high fiber pasta salad the way you like it.

Makes 4–5 servings

- 2 cups high-fiber pasta of your choice (whole wheat, multigrain, quinoa, rice, etc.), preferably the fusilli shape.
- 2 cups chopped or sliced firmer vegetables (such as broccoli, carrots, peas, corn, zucchini, string beans, etc.), slightly cooked
- 1/2 cup chopped fresh tomato
- 2 tablespoons chopped scallions
- 1 cup protein of your choice (cooked meat, poultry, tuna, salmon, etc.) (optional)
- 1 cup beans, cooked from dried *or* canned beans, rinsed and drained (optional)
- 1/3 cup lemon juice or vinegar of your choice
- 2 tablespoons plain yogurt *or* plain greek yogurt
- 2 tablespoons olive oil or oil of your choice
- 2 teaspoons yellow mustard
- 1/4 teaspoon turmeric (optional)
- other seasonings of your choice (garlic powder, paprika, chili powder, dried basil, etc.)

Cook pasta according to package directions. Drain and let cool.

In a large bowl, mix together pasta, vegetables, protein (if using), and beans (if using).

In a separate bowl, mix together remaining ingredients. Pour over pasta mixture and toss.

Chill before serving to allow flavors to blend.

Lentil Citrus Salad

This citrusy salad excites the taste buds and is fiber rich.

Makes 4 servings

2 cups cooked lentils, green or brown
2 scallions, sliced (approximately 2 tablespoons)
2 tablespoons chopped parsley
1 cup orange or tangerine segments
1/4 cup dried cranberries or dried cherries
basil leaves, thinly shredded (optional)
1 tablespoon olive oil or oil of choice
1 tablespoon apple cider vinegar
1/2 teaspoon dry mustard
1/4 teaspoon garlic powder
pinch of dried thyme leaf
pinch of salt

Combine the lentils, scallions, parsley, citrus segments, dried cranberries or dried cherries, and basil (if using) in a large bowl.

In a separate bowl, mix together oil, vinegar, dry mustard, garlic powder, thyme and salt. Pour over the lentil mixture and gently combine.

Serve at room temperature or chilled, depending on your preference

Speedy Garbanzo Bean Salad

Garbanzo beans or chickpeas are loaded with healthy amounts of nutritionally charged vitamins and minerals and are powerful source of fiber. It makes a great main dish or side dish, or it can be eaten in a pita or wrap.

Makes 4 main servings or 6 side-dish servings

- 2 cups garbanzo beans, cooked from dried *or* 1 (15-ounce) can garbanzo beans, rinsed and drained
- 1 1/2 cups chopped tomatoes *or* cherry tomatoes, halved
- 1 cup sliced celery
- 1/2 cup thinly sliced scallions
- 1/2 cup chopped parsley
- 3 tablespoons lemon juice
- 1 tablespoon balsamic vinegar
- 1 tablespoon extra-virgin olive oil or oil of choice
- 1/2 teaspoon garlic powder
- additional seasonings to taste
- feta cheese (optional)

Toss all ingredients except feta in a large bowl and mix together.

Best chilled before serving. Serve sprinkled with feta cheese, if desired.

Variation: Add some coarsely chopped fresh greens, such as kale, chard, basil, or mustard greens.

Red Quinoa Salad Delight

Great for a quick and nutritious lunch or light meal.

Makes 4 servings

- 1/2 cup red quinoa, thoroughly rinsed
- 1 cup vegetable broth or water
- 1/2 cup diced peeled cucumber
- 1/2 cup diced fresh tomato
- 2 tablespoons sliced scallions
- 2 tablespoons minced fresh parsley
- 1 tablespoon extra-virgin olive oil or oil of choice
- 1 tablespoon lemon juice or orange juice
- 1 tablespoon balsamic vinegar
- 1/2 teaspoon garlic powder
- 1/4 teaspoon ground cinnamon
- chopped peppers for spice (optional)
- lemon zest or orange zest for tanginess (optional)

Cook quinoa in broth or water according to package directions. (Can also be cooked in a rice cooker.) Allow to cool to room temperature.

In a large bowl, combine quinoa with remaining ingredients and mix thoroughly.

Chill before serving

Sorghum Salad

Sorghum is an uncommonly used ancient grain; it is a nutritional powerhouse, high in fiber, iron, and protein.

Makes 4–6 servings

- 1/2 cup dried sorghum cooked according to package directions (approximately 2 cups cooked)
- 1 cup cherry tomatoes, halved or quartered
- 1 cup chopped peeled cucumber
- 1/2 cup grated carrot, peeled or unpeeled
- 1/3 cup dried cranberries or dried cherries
- 1/3 cup pumpkin seeds or sesame seeds
- 2 tablespoons lemon juice or vinegar of choice (more if needed)

- 2 tablespoons chopped parsley
- 2 tablespoons chopped scallions
- 2 tablespoons olive oil or oil of choice (more if needed)
- 1 teaspoon garlic powder
- 1/4 teaspoon dried dill weed

Mix all ingredients together in a large bowl. Adjust seasonings according to taste.

Chill before serving.

Variation: Top individual servings with some cubed avocado, sliced strawberries, small slices of tangerine, grated cheese, or beans for a different taste.

Southwestern Salad with Zing

A zippy and snazzy fiber-rich salad

Makes 4–6 servings

- 1 cup cooked barley, brown rice, or other whole grain
- 1 cup black beans, cooked from dried *or* canned black beans, rinsed and drained
- 1 cup frozen corn *or* canned corn, drained
- 1/2 cup chopped fresh basil
- 1/2 cup chopped parsley or cilantro
- 1/2 cup chopped fresh tomatoes *or* canned diced tomatoes, drained (optional)
- 2 scallions, chopped (approximately 3 tablespoons)
- 2 tablespoon red wine vinegar or balsamic vinegar
- 1 tablespoon olive oil or oil of choice
- 1/2 teaspoon ground cumin
- 1/2 teaspoon garlic powder
- 1/4 teaspoon dry mustard
- additional seasonings if desired

Combine all ingredients in a large bowl. Mix well. Adjust seasonings to taste.

For best flavor, cover and refrigerate at least 1 hour before serving to allow flavors to blend.

Variation: add 1/2 cup chopped pepper (any color), 1/2 cup chopped celery, 1/3 cup cubed avocado, paprika, dried thyme leaf, turmeric, lemon or lime juice instead of vinegar

Spelt Salad for a Change

Try spelt, an ancient grain, for a change. The very high fiber content in spelt means that it facilitates digestion in a major way.

Makes approximately 5 servings

- 2 cups cooked spelt (may substitute wheat berries)
- 1 cup black beans, cooked from dried *or* canned black beans, rinsed and drained
- 1/2 cup finely chopped parsley
- 1/2 cup shredded carrot
- 1/2 cup diced celery
- 1/2 cup peeled and diced cucumber
- 1/2 cup diced fresh tomato (more if desired)
- 2 tablespoons chopped scallions
- 2 tablespoons lemon juice
- 1 tablespoon dried cranberries or dried cherries
- 1 tablespoon diced dried apricots
- 1 tablespoon lemon zest
- 1 tablespoon olive oil or oil of choice
- 1/2 teaspoon ground cumin
- 1/2 teaspoon garlic powder
- 1/4 teaspoon ground ginger
- other seasonings as desired
- diced bell pepper (optional)

Mix all ingredients together in a large bowl. Refrigerate at least 30 minutes before serving to allow flavors to blend.

Variation: Add diced poultry, meat, or seafood for more protein and to make the dish more savory.

Sweet Corn, Black Beans, and Tomato Salad

This is a flavorful and colorful salad. It is hearty enough to be eaten alone, or it makes a great side dish for grilled chicken or fish.

Makes 4–5 servings

- 2 cups cherry tomatoes, halved or quartered *or* scant 2 cups diced fresh tomatoes (approximately 2 large)
- 1 1/2 cups black beans, cooked from dried *or* 1 (14-ounce) can black beans, drained and rinsed
- 1 cup sweet corn, frozen or scraped from cooked fresh ears
- 1/2 cup grated carrot
- 1/2 cup diced red bell pepper (optional)

- 1/4 cup chopped red onions or green onions
- 3 tablespoons chopped cilantro, parsley, basil, or kale
- 2 tablespoons lime juice or lemon juice
- 1 tablespoon extra-virgin olive oil or oil of choice
- 1 1/2 teaspoons ground cumin
- 1 teaspoon red wine vinegar
- 1/2 teaspoon garlic powder
- zest of one lime
- salt and pepper to taste
- additional seasonings to taste (optional)

Mix all ingredients together in a large bowl and serve at room temperature or chilled.

Wheat Berry Citrus-Orange Salad

Wheat berries have a sweet, nutty flavor and hold their shape even after long cooking. They are a powerful source of fiber, proteins, and B vitamins.

Makes 4 servings

1 cup wheat berries (also called whole-grain wheat or whole-grain wheat kernels), rinsed and soaked overnight
1 1/2 cups navel oranges, peeled and sectioned
2/3 cup chopped parsley or cilantro
1/2 cup sliced celery
1/4 cup minced red onion (more or less depending on preference)
3 tablespoons lemon juice
1 tablespoon olive oil or oil of choice
pepper to taste (optional)

Drain and rinse soaked wheat berries. Add to a medium size pot with approximately 3 cups water. Bring water to a boil.

Reduce heat and simmer covered until wheat berries are tender and water is absorbed (approximately 1 1/2–2 hours). Let stand for 10 minutes. Pour off any remaining water.

Combine wheat berries with remaining ingredients in a large bowl.

Refrigerate at least 1 hour before serving.

Tip: If you are not serving this salad the same day, keep the wheat berries and other ingredients stored separately in the refrigerator for optimal texture. Combine the day you are serving the salad.

Variation: Add some shredded carrots for a different taste and look.

White Bean Salad

Light and quick bean salad.

Makes 2–3 servings

- 1 cup white beans (great northern, cannellini or small white), cooked from dried *or* canned white beans, rinsed and drained
- 1 cup chopped fresh tomatoes *or* cherry tomatoes, halved
- 1/2 cup chopped fresh parsley or cilantro
- 1/3 cup minced red onion
- 1 tablespoon lemon juice
- 1 tablespoon balsamic vinegar
- 1/4 teaspoon garlic powder
- 1–2 tablespoons of oil of choice for more flavor (optional)
- dash of salt (optional)

Mix all ingredients together in a large bowl.

Serve immediately or chill covered in refrigerator first.

White Beans and Seafood Salad

The beans and seafood blend well for a tasty, easy, fiber-rich dish

Makes 3 servings, approximately 2/3 cup each

- 1 (6-ounce) can tuna, salmon, or crabmeat, drained
- 2/3 cup white beans of any type, cooked from dried *or* canned white beans, rinsed and drained
- 1/4 cup raisins or dried cranberries
- 1/4 cup torn or chopped fresh parsley, cilantro, or basil
- 1 tablespoon lemon juice
- zest of 1/2 lemon (approximately 1 1/2 teaspoons; use more if you want more lemony flavor)
- pepper (optional)
- other seasonings as desired

Gently mix all ingredients together in a large bowl.

Chill before serving if time permits.

Variation: Add 1/3 cup chopped celery, 1/3 cup chopped cucumber, finely chopped scallions or red onion, 1–2 tablespoons olive oil or oil of choice, and 1/2 teaspoon dijon mustard. Use them individually or in combination.

Basic Tabbouleh Salad with Variations

It's best to make this salad ahead of time to allow time for the flavors to blend.

Serving size approximately 1 cup

- 1 cup bulgur wheat
- 2 cups boiling water

In a medium bowl, pour boiling water over bulgur. Stir. Cover and let stand approximately 60 minutes.

Drain excess liquid. Fluff bulgur. Allow bulgur to cool.

Once cooled, add other ingredients and mix.

Blueberry Version

- 1 cup fresh or frozen blueberries
- 1/2 cup chopped kale
- 1/4 cup chopped nuts of choice.
- 2 tablespoons chopped parsley or cilantro
- 1 tablespoon olive oil or oil of choice

Bean Version

- 1 or more cups canned beans of choice, rinsed and drained *or* beans, cooked from dried
- 1/2 cup chopped dried fruit, such as apricots
- curry powder, garlic powder, or ground ginger to taste
- chopped scallions (optional)
- olive oil or oil of choice to taste (optional)

- vinegar of choice to taste (optional)

Seafood Version

- 2 cups chunks of salmon or other seafood
- 1 cup chopped tomatoes
- 1 cup chopped artichoke hearts, canned, frozen, or jarred (optional)
- 1/2 cup chopped peeled cucumber
- 2 tablespoons chopped scallions
- olive oil or oil of choice to taste
- lemon juice to taste.
- seasonings of choice to taste

Fruit Version

- approximately 1 1/2 cups slices or chunks of fresh fruit, like peaches, nectarines, figs, apricots, strawberries, oranges, or watermelon
- balsamic vinegar to taste
- olive oil or oil of choice to taste
- 1/3 cup chopped parsley
- chopped nuts and feta or goat cheese for topping (optional)

Poultry Version

- 1 1/2 cups diced cooked chicken or turkey
- 1 cup diced peeled cucumber
- 2 tablespoons chopped scallions
- 2 tablespoons chopped parsley or cilantro
- 1–2 tablespoons olive oil or oil of choice
- small amount of orange juice to taste

Note: For added flavor, add some fresh fruit from the fruit version just before serving.

Chickpea (Garbanzo Bean) Tabbouleh

This recipe combines two powerful fiber sources

Makes 4–6 servings

- 1/2 cup bulgur wheat
- 1 cup coarsely chopped parsley or more if desired
- 1 cup canned garbanzo beans, rinsed and drained *or* garbanzo beans, cooked from dried
- 1 cup diced fresh or canned tomatoes *or* 1 cup chopped mango, fresh or frozen
- 1/2 cup chopped red onion or scallions
- 1/2 cup peeled and diced cucumber
- 1/4 cup lemon juice or lime juice
- 2 tablespoons olive oil or oil of choice
- 1/2 teaspoon ground cumin
- 1/2 teaspoon ground cinnamon
- 1/2 teaspoon garlic powder
- 1/4 teaspoon salt
- 1/8 teaspoon cayenne pepper
- dash pepper
- 1/2 cup diced red, orange, or yellow bell pepper (optional)
- 3 tablespoons chopped mint (optional)
- feta cheese for topping (optional)

Rinse bulgur and place in a small bowl. Pour 1 cup boiling water over bulgur. Cover and let it stand 30–60 minutes.

Drain excess liquid. Fluff bulgur. Place bulgur in a large bowl and allow bulgur to cool.

Meanwhile, combine chickpeas, mangoes or tomatoes, onions, cucumber, parsley, lemon or lime juice, oil, cumin, cinnamon, garlic powder, salt, and cayenne pepper.

Gently combine with bulgur wheat. Add bell pepper and mint, if using.

Refrigerate at least 1 hour to let flavors blend. Sprinkle some feta cheese on top if desired.

May be served stuffed into pita halves and topped with hummus or dressing.

Cucumber Tabbouleh

Bulgur is a good source of fiber, protein, iron, and vitamin B-6

Makes 6 servings

- 1 cup bulgur
- 2 cups boiling water
- 1 1/2 cups peeled and diced cucumber
- 1 cup chopped fresh parsley or cilantro
- 2 medium fresh tomatoes, seeded and chopped
- 2 scallions, finely chopped
- 1/4 cup olive oil or oil of choice (may want to use less)
- 3 tablespoons lime or lemon juice
- black pepper to taste
- garlic powder to taste

Pour boiling water over bulgur in a large bowl and allow to soak 30 minutes.

Drain excess liquid. Fluff bulgur and allow bulgur to cool.

Dry bulgur thoroughly (otherwise salad will be soggy).

Add remaining ingredients. Toss well and serve at room temperature.

Quinoa Tabbouleh

Pack some for a nutritious lunch.

Makes approximately 5 servings, 1 cup each

- 1 1/2 cups water
- 1 cup uncooked quinoa, rinsed well
- 1/2 cup coarsely chopped fresh tomato
- 1/2 cup chopped fresh cilantro or parsley *or* 2 tablespoons dried parsley flakes
- 1/3 cup peeled and chopped cucumber
- 1/3 cup dried cranberries or golden raisins
- 1/3 cup fresh lemon juice or lime juice
- 3 tablespoons chopped scallions
- 1 tablespoon olive oil or oil of choice
- 1/2 teaspoon salt, or to taste
- 1/4 teaspoon pepper, or to taste
- other seasonings, such as garlic powder, turmeric, or ground cumin (optional)

Combine water and quinoa in a saucepan, and bring to a boil. Reduce heat. Cover and simmer approximately 20 minutes, or until all liquid is absorbed. Remove from heat. Fluff with a fork. (Alternately, quinoa may be cooked in a rice cooker.)

Stir in the rest of the remaining ingredients. Cover and let mixture stand at room temperature 20 minutes to allow flavors to blend.

Serve at room temperature or chilled.

Variation: Add another source of protein.

Seafood Tabbouleh

Quick and easy. Eat as is, or serve tabbouleh wrapped in a whole wheat tortilla or pita or on lettuce leaves.

Makes 3–4 servings

1/2 cup bulgur wheat
1 cup chopped fresh tomato
2/3–1 cup peeled and chopped cucumber
1/2 cup chopped cilantro or parsley
1 (6-ounce) or (7-ounce) can water-packed tuna or salmon, drained and flaked
1/3 cup chopped scallions
2 tablespoons olive oil or oil of choice
2 tablespoons lemon juice
garlic powder and other spices to taste
small amount of chopped red bell pepper (optional)

In a medium bowl, pour 1 cup boiling water over bulgur wheat. Cover and let soak 10 minutes. Pour off excess water, and squeeze bulgur wheat dry.

Add remaining ingredients and mix well. Fluff with a fork.

Let mixture set awhile to blend flavors before serving.

Tabbouleh with a Fruity Twist

The beans in this recipe add fiber, and the fruit increases the nutrition and flavor.

Makes 4–6 servings

3/4 cup bulgur wheat
1 1/2 cups boiling water
1 (15-ounce) can black beans or garbanzo beans, rinsed and drained *or* 2 cups beans, cooked from dried
1 1/2 cups coarsely chopped watermelon without seeds *or* coarsely chopped mango, fresh or frozen
1/2 cup chopped parsley
2 scallions, chopped (approximately 1/4 cup)
3 tablespoons lemon juice
1 tablespoon lemon zest
1–2 tablespoon olive oil or oil of choice
1/2 teaspoon ground cinnamon
1/2 teaspoon garlic powder
1/4 teaspoon ground cumin
additional spices as desired
feta cheese or goat cheese for topping (optional)

Pour boiling water over bulgur. Let stand covered 30 minutes.

Drain off any water. Fluff with a fork, and let stand uncovered until cool, approximately 15–30 minutes more.

Place cooled bulgur in a bowl with remaining ingredients except cheese, and gently mix.

Cool in refrigerator awhile to allow flavors to blend.

Sprinkle on cheese and serve.

CPSIA information can be obtained
at www.ICGtesting.com
Printed in the USA
BVHW021750090620
580874BV00009B/28

9 781524 652432